The Power of Positive Criticism

The Power of Positive Criticism

Hendrie Weisinger, Ph.D.

AMACOM

American Management Association

New York • Atlanta • Boston • Chicago • Kansas City • San Francisco • Washington, D.C.
Brussels • Mexico City • Tokyo • Toronto

Special discounts on bulk quantities of AMACOM books are available to corporations, professional associations, and other organizations. For details, contact Special Sales Department, AMACOM, an imprint of AMA Publications, a division of American Management Association, 1601 Broadway, New York, NY 10019.
Tel.: 212-903-8316. Fax: 212-903-8083.

This publication is designed to provide accurate and authoritative information in regard to the subject matter covered. It is sold with the understanding that the publisher is not engaged in rendering legal, accounting, or other professional service. If legal advice or other expert assistance is required, the services of a competent professional person should be sought.

Library of Congress Cataloging-in-Publication Data

Weisinger, Hendrie.
    The power of positive criticism / Hendrie Weisinger.
        p.   cm.
    Includes index.
    ISBN 0-8144-0483-9
    1. Criticism, Personal.   2. Psychology, Industrial.   I. Title.
    BF637.C74W45   1999
    158.2—dc21
                                                        99–34293
                                                            CIP

Printing number

10   9   8   7

This book is dedicated to the New York Yankees, who, for more than forty years, have provided me with hundreds of thrills, some chills, inspiration, and motivation, and have often helped me escape the harsh realities of life.

Contents

Section II: Frequent, Challenging, and
Difficult Criticism Situations   95

Acknowledgments

After writing six books, I can now say that I have assembled a team comparable to the '27, '61, and '98 Yankees. Let it be said that I have a rich pool of talent to draw upon, and the fact is, having so many supportive people in my corner makes competition to be one of my twenty-seven team members severe, to say nothing of what it takes to be a starter. Thus, to all those who have helped me and are not mentioned, I still appreciate your enthusiasm toward my work and me. Here is the starting nine:

First Base: Lee Sachs. A veteran of the team for more than thirty years, Lee has proved to be an iron man of support. Gives me excellent advice, has a great eye for value, and makes very few errors.

Second Base: Eric Koch. Like Richardson, extremely reliable, sure-handed, and will come up big. Always encouraging and applauds my big hits.

Shortstop: Steve Gold. Similar to Kubek: quiet and steady. Very good in the clutch, and is my canoe companion. Excellent for getting me in a good mood.

Third Base: Richard Greene. Richard, who was a top wiffle ball prospect, has been on the team for more than forty years. He brings a lot of humor, and knows how to keep me loose. Has the best handwriting of any team member, and will not fold in the clutch.

Left Field: Alan Driefus. A long-time veteran, Alan helped me wrestle out many problems. On road trips, he always makes the effort to make the long haul from left field to where I am playing.

Right Field: Mel Kinder. Despite his loss in speed and power, Mel continues to come through in situations that require novel ideas. In a way, he has moved from Maris to Bauer.

Center Field: Lenny Levine. Pulls the outfield together by combining the power of the Mick with the grace of Dimag. Always thoughtful and loving to my family and me, Lenny is very close to hitting one out of the stadium.

The Battery:

Catching: Kenny Cinnamon. There is no better catcher of feelings, and he knows how to call the game. Always thinking an inning ahead, Kenny is a Berra-Dickey combination. Will not allow any passed balls, and will not allow a wild pitch, and packs plenty of power. He commands the infield by letting them know who's the boss.

Pitching: Ron Podell. With Ron on the mound, it is hard not to feel confident. He knows how to pitch in any situation, and can throw it from any direction. With Catfish control and Ford craftiness, Podell will always figure out a way to help me get the win. Will throw the shutout, but only if he has to. Will also throw the spitter if necessary.

Designated Hitter: Simon Klebenow. A recent addition, Sy has already proved himself to be valuable, and has helped me score big.

Bullpen: Closer Howard Norman. From Los Angeles to Washington to Texas, Howard has helped me put out the fires. Like Shantz, Arroyo, and Rivera, knows how to focus when the heat is on.

Bench: Because of space limitations, I can only list the bench players who help make my team awesome: Wharton, Penn State, Cornell, RPI, NYU, IMS, the University of California, Lorie Weisinger, Thelma Weisinger, Ronnie Fagin, Elliot Macht, Sandy

Billings, Kenny Shapiro, The Learning Circle, and the Young Presidents Organization.

Bat Boy: Danny Weisinger. My team would always be incomplete without him.

Cheerleader: Bri Weisinger. She adds cheer to my life.

Biggest Team Change: After careful evaluation, it was determined that the Meisner boys need to go back to Triple A for more seasoning in social graces and clarification of vocational interests. All team members hope they return for the seventh book.

Overview: With the starting nine providing a wealth of support and enthusiasm, backed by incredible bench strength, I should have a first-place finish. The only possible source of team conflict would be Richard Greene consistently defeating Ron Podell in golf.

Introduction

I had just finished a short conference presentation to a major financial institution on the subject of giving and taking criticism. The president of the company came up to offer me a congratulatory handshake; as he did, he remarked, "I never realized criticism was such a complex, important, essential, and powerful process."

Since I had been studying the subject of criticism for over twenty years, ever since my interest in the subject was sparked by witnessing a staff psychiatrist destructively criticize a fellow graduate student in front of her peers, the president's comment was an understatement to me.

Criticism is complex. The words you choose to use, the moods and emotions of both parties, the nature of the relationship you have with the giver or the receiver, the content of the criticism, and the time and the place, mixed with many other variables, make giving and taking criticism a very complex and difficult task. And there is an abundance of research that indicates most people do not do this task well.

Criticism is important. Acts and situations that are worthy of criticism are acts and situations that need to be evaluated because they affect our welfare. At work, behavior that is criticized is thought to relate to productivity. In society, acts and situations that are criticized are thought to affect our daily living; therefore, they deserve to be evaluated. Pick up the newspaper or listen to the news, and you will hear daily stories about someone or something being criticized. In this context, the news is telling us that these are the people who are worthy of criticism, these are the important events and behaviors that shape our days and thus deserve a closer look. Criticism is important because it tells us *what* is important.

Criticism is essential. Performance appraisal, team functioning, quality control, customer service, leadership and management development, and managing conflict are all daily organizational tasks that drive the welfare of an organization. In each of these tasks, giving and taking criticism is an essential and underlying factor as to how well the task is performed. For example, you cannot have an effective team unless team members can give and take criticism to and from each other. If an executive cannot take criticism, or if those close to her are ineffective in giving it to her, she has little chance of developing herself or her leadership skills. Customer service is all about soliciting criticism from customers for the purpose of giving better service. Furthermore, no job is criticism-exempt. Criticism at work is a common denominator for all of us.

And, of course, criticism is powerful. It can make or break careers. It can help an organization flourish or flounder. It is also powerful in that it evokes strong feelings and emotions ranging from anger to enthusiasm. It is powerful enough to affect our attitude toward work and those who work with us. In short, criticism is so powerful that it impacts just about every aspect of our work experience.

But the purpose of this book is not to make the case that criticism has these attributes. I'll summarize that case by simply pointing out that the last twenty years have provided us with a tremendous amount of empirical research that clearly indicates that giving and taking criticism in a positive manner is crucial to individual and organizational success. Success is defined in a broad sense, including job enjoyment, better working relationships, better mental health, improved self-esteem, increased productivity, and greater results.

With that in mind, the purpose of this book is to help you develop your skill in using the power of positive criticism. When you do this, you will be using criticism as a tool to motivate, educate, develop, teach, and build relationships.

To use criticism in this manner is in accordance with criticism's original purpose—a neutral, objective appraisal of ideas and actions. The Greeks used the word *kritikos*, "able to discern or judge." One who criticized was expected to assess the merits as well as the demerits of an object or situation, and to make judgments accordingly. The goals of criticism were to communicate, to influence, and to motivate.

Criticism of that sort played an important and positive role in the evaluation process: It helped one look realistically at one's aims and actions; it pointed the way toward new resources and skills; it increased one's tolerance for a variety of opinions. But over the years—and for many reasons—this concept of criticism became skewed until, finally, only the negative connotations of the word remained.

This book helps you use criticism as it was originally intended; when you do, you will ignite the best in yourself, others, and your organization.

Furthermore, as you use the power of positive criticism, you will be dramatically more successful in the broadest sense of the word.

What to Expect

The Power of Positive Criticism is organized into two main sections. Section I consists of twenty tips that will help you get the power of positive criticism.

The "Tips in Action" chapter illustrates how applying the tips transforms an initially negative criticism into a positive criticism.

Section II contains the most difficult criticism encounters that occur on the job. For each situation, the underlying factors that make the situation difficult are discussed; then practical, proven-effective criticism methods, techniques, and interventions are provided to help you manage each situation.

The book concludes with observations about the kind of people who consistently get the positive power of criticism.

There is also an appendix, which provides you with a useful support tool, The Criticism Inventory (TCI), that will make it easier for you to apply and benefit from *The Power of Positive Criticism.*

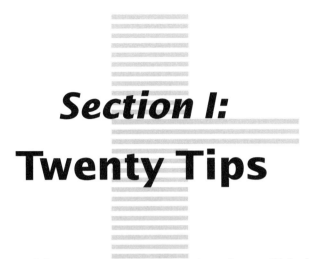

Section I:

Twenty Tips

Section I provides you with twenty tips that will help you harness the power of positive criticism. The tips are based on three sources—theories, research, and clinical experiences. Together, they combine to give you proven, practical ways for enhancing your skill in giving and taking criticism.

Each tip reflects different aspects and factors that influence the criticism process. All of the tips can be applied to both giving and receiving criticism, although some are geared more toward giving and some more toward receiving criticism. Sometimes, integrating one tip into your criticisms will do the job; other times, you will have to use a combination of several to get the results you desire.

Blending, integrating, and adapting the tips to your criticism encounters is how you get the power of positive criticism.

Tip #1:

Befriend Criticism

Criticism comes with the job. Any job. It doesn't matter whether you are a president, teacher, banker, baker, baseball player, salesperson, construction worker, architect, secretary, consultant, government official, chauffeur, pilot, or postman. Criticism comes with your job. And since it does, you might as well befriend it so that you can make it work for you.

Unfortunately, the overwhelming majority of working people find this to be a most difficult task. Many say unreasonable. Indeed, I've started out a hundred seminars by asking participants: "How many of you come home each day and say to your significant other, 'Gee, I had a great day today. I got criticized.' " While there are many chuckles, few hands go up. I follow up: "What makes it difficult to befriend criticism? What's so bad about being criticized?"

Chances are, if you are like these working folks, your answer is along the lines of: "Criticism is negative." "It means I've done something wrong, that I have to change." "I am not as good as I think I am." "It points out my flaws." "It means I am not doing my job."

And now on the other side of the coin. "How many of you like to give criticism?" As before, few, if any, raise their hands. I ask, "What's so bad about having to criticize someone?" Now plenty of hands go up: "I don't want to hurt their feelings." "I don't have the right to criticize them." "I don't know how they will respond." "No purpose." "I don't want to cause a problem." "I'm afraid of how they might respond."

When I hear responses such as these, I understand why so many people have difficulty giving and taking criticism: They think of criticism negatively.

It's a well-known psychological fact that your thoughts influence how you feel and how you act. Academics use the phrase *cognitive appraisal,* a mental process that helps us to define what is happening to or around us. Its roots lie in the special qualities and circumstances—family background, natural talents, physical appearance and health, systems of belief, fears and hopes—that shape our personalities. These combine to form the basis for the unique way each of us interprets our surroundings, gives meaning to outside events, and appraises the situations we encounter at home and at work.

How we interpret any situation obviously will vary with the circumstances, but the point is: However we appraise it triggers the feelings and behavior that follow.

How do you *appraise* criticism? Again, if your responses are similar to those of seminar participants, it is safe to assume you have a negative appraisal of criticism: You evaluate criticism as a negative, and this negative evaluation of criticism dictates that you will almost always experience distressed feelings and act counterproductive to your interests. Of course, the more you experience criticism as a negative, the more apt you are to respond to criticism in a negative manner. Because criticism is so frequent, you will inevitably find that the mere thought of your presentation being criticized by your team members creates high anxiety.

It is at this point that many individuals, especially those in human resources functions or organizational training and development positions, raise the issue that since most people think of criticism as negative, why even use the word. A different word, they argue, should be used. The popular choice is the more benign "feedback." In fact, I have encountered some individuals and organizations that feel so strongly about this point that they have banned the word "criticism" from their work culture vocabulary.

But does this really make sense? Let me give you two reasons that make it essential to call criticism "criticism." First, it is obviously your choice to call criticism whatever you want. Let's say you opt for feedback. I come up to you: "Hey, I got some feedback for you about your presentation (or suggestions, or pointers)." Now I get on with giving you "feedback."

But I cannot control your thoughts; after a few seconds of hearing my feedback, they become: "Wait a second; he is not giving me feedback. He is criticizing me." And since you have a negative definition of criticism, you can see how the encounter will take a drastic turn for the worse, even though I am using the word feedback.

In other words, since you and those around you are going to give criticism and be criticized, you might as well use the word "criticism" because doing so allows you and others the opportunity to learn how to "befriend" the concept.

Using the word "feedback" and avoiding the word "criticism" does the opposite: It perpetuates the message that criticism is negative. By denying or avoiding use of the word, you rob the individual of the opportunity to learn how to deal with criticism when he experiences criticism. Better to hear criticism as criticism and learn to appreciate it. Calling it something else does not make the act of criticizing go away. The Emperor is still wearing no clothes.

The second reason why it is essential to call criticism "criticism" is based on criticism's characteristic that distinguishes it from those other corporate vernacular replacements—feedback, executive coaching, mentoring. Criticism is the only word that refers to evaluation.

When you read your coworker's marketing report, your job is not to give feedback or coach the report—it is to evaluate it, to criticize it. When you give a performance appraisal, you are asked to give your evaluation. When you are being criticized, you feel as if you are being evaluated—and you are.

We all need evaluative information. We need to know how we are doing, and we need to let other people know how they are doing. We all have stories to prove this point to be true.

Thus, criticism deals with the communication of evaluative information; this is why acknowledging criticism as criticism is so important. It is through evaluative information that we gain awareness about ourselves. It is through evaluative information that we develop and promote ourselves. It is through evaluative information that we formulate what decisions to make, what actions to take.

Evaluative information is crucial for learning, and this is what makes criticism so essential to individual and organizational effectiveness—criticism is a learning mechanism.

To exile the word "criticism" from a corporate vocabulary, and thus its culture, prevents the organization and its individuals from valuing evaluative information. By calling it something else (feedback, for example) ignores the importance of criticism, and this almost always brings negative results.

To get the power of positive criticism, you must first befriend it. This does not simply mean remaining nondefensive when someone criticizes you or playing mental gymnastics with words so you can hear your critic's message productively. These skills are necessary but insufficient.

Befriending criticism is a more substantial task. It requires a re-psycholization—an internalization of the belief that criticism is a requirement for you to be successful. The end result is that you come to value criticism.

How exactly do you befriend criticism? The easiest way is to take steps that will help you *reappraise* criticism in a manner that is more in line with its historical roots.

To do this, I strongly suggest that you take two actions. (Over the years, you probably have developed a hardening of the corollaries so you need to take action to overcome your thoughts.)

First, write down a positive criticism message on a three-by-five card (a sign would be better) and put that card in a high-visibility location. Every time you (and others) see it, you will be reinforcing your reappraisal of criticism as a positive. Examples you could use are:

> "Criticism is information that can help me grow."
> "Criticism is teaching appropriate skills and knowledge."

This might sound hokey, but I can assure you that it will be effective in changing how you think about criticism, and thus how you give and receive it.

The second step is a little more difficult but extremely rewarding. You are to actively solicit criticism from others. Take this step wisely. Do not ask for criticism; others' negative perception of criticism will cause them to tell you what you are doing wrong or view you as being sarcastic or condescending.

Instead, sincerely ask them for their thoughts on how you can be more effective. And then, if you can do it with sincerity, thank them for their "criticism." Using the C word here will begin to transform their appraisal of criticism into a positive action, and your soliciting of their evaluations will give you practice in befriending criticism.

These two steps support each other. The more you think of criticism as a positive, the easier it is to solicit. The more you benefit from soliciting criticism, the more natural it becomes for you to appraise criticism positively.

And once you befriend criticism, it will reciprocate—it will befriend you with its positive power!

Tip #2:

Criticize Strategically

Having a corporate strategy is usually a top priority. Unfortunately, having a criticism strategy is not. It's been my experience that few people report taking time to plan out exactly what they want to say and how they want to say it. The usual modus operandi is to express the thoughts as you feel them—which is usually negative.

How about you? Are you a *strategic* criticizer? Recount the last time you criticized a coworker. How much time did you actually take in preparing your thoughts before you offered them? Or did you criticize off-the-cuff with spontaneous negative remarks—caustic, sarcastic, blaming, or accusatory "you are wrong" statements—that produced resentment instead of improvement?

People who consistently tap into the power of positive criticism are strategic: They actively take responsibility for how they communicate. They see themselves as a directive force, with the goal being to get their recipient to take their criticism productively. They recognize that the communication process itself is influential and that the more active they become in it, the more they can influence how their recipient responds.

Having this active philosophy is crucial because it entails advance planning—it forces you to become aware of what you want to accomplish, what you are actually going to say, and how you are going to say it.

With this awareness, you give yourself the opportunity

to "hear your criticisms" and decide whether or not you are going about it in the best way.

Many people point out that they do not have the time to plan in advance how they can best criticize someone. It is indeed true that things happen on the job that demand an immediate response. And because of the spontaneity and emotionality of the situation, we are caught off guard. Our destructive patterns of criticizing quickly emerge, making the situation worse.

Fortunately, we also know of specific times at work in which we frequently have to point out a wrongdoing. When I pose the question to a group of sales managers, "How many of you know situations in advance in which you will have to give criticism?" almost everybody raises their hands.

Most sales managers have a pretty good idea of the criticisms they will eventually have to give their new sales recruits. The same is true for a supervisor of student teachers, nurses, or flight attendants. These situations, the criticisms we know we are going to have to give, provide us with a rich opportunity to develop our criticism skills.

The sales manager who knows he is going to have to criticize his subordinate's first-time sales presentation for being too long and impersonal can begin to think, "How can I say this so that he will be most receptive." The nurse who knows she will have to tell her student practitioner that he is neglecting his patient's need to talk will be able to plan in advance the best way to do it. When the moment of truth comes, they are ready. Instead of blurting out destructive comments, they can make their point skillfully because of their preparation and thus positively influence behavior. At the very least, their strategic thinking prevents them from making the situation worse.

What is the trick to becoming a strategic criticizer so that you can use the power of positive criticism? Your best bet is to practice by identifying a situation in which you are required to give criticism. Before you give the criticism, ask yourself the following questions:

- ◊ Exactly what do I want to communicate?
- ◊ What do I want to change?
- ◊ What are my motives for expressing this criticism? (If a subordinate's performance made you look bad, you may be angrily passing down your boss's criticism in a nonproductive manner. Beware of those times when your motive is to get even.)
- ◊ What specific solutions and goals can I offer, and what can I do to help the person achieve these goals?

You will also get yourself in the habit of being a strategic criticizer by making a checklist of key questions that you find helpful to ask yourself before you give criticism. If you faithfully use your checklist, you will automatically ask yourself those questions in future criticism situations.

What about those unforeseen situations that require an immediate response? All you need to do is to remember that before you give the criticism—whether it is to a subordinate, coworker, team member, client, or customer—ask yourself the strategic question: "How can I communicate this information so the person will be receptive?" Inevitably, your answer will help you get the power of positive criticism.

Tip #3:

Be Improvement-Oriented

It's intrinsic. It is part of your nature. I'm speaking about your desire to want to improve, to want to do better. Vocational theorists and psychological research tell us that people want to do their best in tasks that are meaningful to them. Use your own experience to validate this point.

For example, if you love to play golf, I'm sure you do not need a pro to tell you to play your best, although you will want the pro to tell you *how* to play your best. If you love to cook, I'm sure you try to make the dish as tasty as possible, although you may need a recipe book and a few cooking lessons to satisfy your taste buds.

The problem is that, for many of us, our desire to improve is stifled by the criticisms we receive. Why? Because most of the criticisms we receive (or give) place a strong emphasis on the negatives (if you have a negative appraisal of criticism). The criticized behavior is usually defined as irrevocable. The recipient is told what he did, thus placing the action in the past; any chance of change for the better is precluded. Since there seems to be little chance for improvement, the recipient, in order to protect his self-esteem, defends his actions rather than looking for ways to improve. The criticism loses its positive power.

Furthermore, whether or not one feels that people lack

an inherent wish to improve, the fact remains that a constant barrage of negative criticism will undermine any recipient's confidence, making it difficult for him to believe he can do the job. Interest is diminished. Many educators and much educational research testify to the point that negative criticism (emphasizing the negatives) given to a child in a particular subject will not only turn her off to that specific subject but will also turn her off to trying to master and explore other areas.

Similarly, the sales manager who, after observing three presentations of the new sales recruit, only emphasizes the negatives of each of her presentations, is doing a good job of convincing the new recruit that she is in the wrong line of work. Her apathy will soon become apparent and, of course, will draw more negative criticism from her manager. This is a bit ironic considering the fact that the history of criticism tells us that one of criticism's most important functions is to help one improve.

Do you—and those you work with—emphasize the negatives when it comes to criticism? Just think about the last three times you were the giver or the taker of criticism. If you find that the negatives are continually emphasized, then you can help yourself, those you work with, and your organization become more productive by making your criticisms improvement-oriented.

Making criticism improvement-oriented creates the mental set of using criticism as a teaching and educational tool. The task becomes to figure out, "How can she do it better? How can I help her improve?" You begin to formulate specific ways in which you can help the recipient. You become solution-oriented.

One way to make criticism improvement-oriented is to move the criticism forward, into the future. Emphasize what the recipient is doing or can do, not what he did. Instead of telling your new recruit, "You did a poor job in presenting the data," which is sure to prompt recipient defensiveness, try, "In your next presentation, use better overheads to show the data. It will help clarify your points."

The latter improvement-oriented criticism not only offers a helpful action to take but focuses on the fact that your new recruit is going to get another chance; you communicate the confidence-building message, "I trust you to succeed."

Change becomes possible because you stress how the recipient can do it better next time. And this lets the recipient feel secure in knowing she will get another chance. She can also feel confident because her critic believes she has the ability to do the job. With this in mind, your trainee can begin to focus her energy on improving her future performance rather than on defending past results. Criticism becomes a put-up instead of a put-down.

Tip #4:

Protect the Self-Esteem

I heard an advertising director tell his assistant, "You should have made the layout less crowded, you didn't use the right colors, and your concept makes no sense."

I heard a manager criticize his sales rep with "You blew it. You need to pay attention to your prospect. You didn't listen. Perhaps you're not right for this job."

Criticisms like these may be improvement-oriented, but they attack the self-esteem—they emphasize that the recipient didn't do well and imply that he might not have the ability to do better. These messages stab the ego.

"Sticks and stones may break my bones, but words will never hurt me" runs the proverb. But if ever a proverb was wide of its mark, this one is. As the majority of people would ruefully admit, words can do more lasting damage than most physical blows. And the words that can do the most damage often come through criticism.

Indeed, criticism and self-esteem have a long and intimate relationship, and it is the closeness of the relationship that gives criticism the power to affect self-esteem for better or for worse. A brief elaboration condensing self-esteem theory and research is in order.

Paradoxically, one's concept of one's self does not develop from the inside out but rather is fashioned from the outside in. "O, wad some power the giftie gie us/To see oursels as others see us!" Robert Burns exclaimed. But that is precisely the way we do see ourselves. It is how we think we appear to others, and how others judge us, that is largely responsible for the self-esteem we develop.

Beginning with the earliest comments from mother and father, the child processes what she sees and hears—specific words, gestures, facial expressions, voice tone—to determine whether the significant others are giving a positive or negative message. These interpretations become the basis of self-esteem.

If significant others give the child an abundance of conventional criticism—emphasizing the negative—the child inevitably begins to build a self-image that is deficient in confidence and satisfaction with herself.

Furthermore, the child begins to evaluate her own performance (even when positive) in the same way that those around her do—emphasizing the negatives or the demerits of the situation.

The results of these two factors, negative criticisms from significant others and negative self-criticism, give birth to low self-esteem. And believe me when I say that low self-esteem handicaps you.

While high self-esteem provides the impetus to try new and challenging behaviors, initiate relationships with others, and quickly bounce back from the setbacks of life one encounters, low self-esteem does the opposite. It makes you approach any new task or assignment with trepidation. It makes it difficult for you to establish relationships, whether it is with your coworkers or clients. It makes adversity more difficult for you to conquer. And most important, it makes you feel bad.

There is another problem too, one which makes criticizing an individual with low self-esteem a very difficult task.

By the time the individual with low self-esteem enters the workforce, his low self-esteem has taught him to handle criticism in one of two ways. First, out of habit all criticism is heard as further validation of being a loser. Negative thoughts quickly emerge, and the criticism is never really evaluated for its merit; it is simply processed as a negative message. Low self-esteem perpetuates itself.

The second way a person with low self-esteem perceives criticism is as an attack that must be warded off. Here, the self-esteem dictates a behavioral repertoire that includes excuses, retaliation, emotional outbursts, and other reactions that rarely serve you well.

In either case, low self-esteem has prevented its holder from taking advantage of one of criticism's most important functions: *a learning mechanism that allows one to develop self-awareness by accurately understanding how one is perceived by others.* It is this awareness that allows one to make changes for the better.

But here is the good news. Low self-esteem is not determined by DNA. It is malleable—if you use the power of positive criticism. Essentially, this means giving criticism in a way that protects the self-esteem. When criticism protects the self-esteem, it becomes more productive because the likelihood that the recipient will process the information with an open mind is increased. The self-esteem has less reason to defend itself when it is not attacked or put down. If the criticism does not threaten or attack, the already-established negative Pavlovian defensive reaction is short-circuited. This frees the recipient to respond differently and more productively. The recipient is able to use the information in a way that helps him learn about himself and, equally important, take actions that will improve his performance. Self-esteem is enhanced, and with it the individual does better in the game of life.

How can you protect someone's self-esteem when giving criticism? First, the most obvious way is to avoid derogatory names and comments that make up so many of our daily criticisms. When criticisms are derogatory, they are perceived as a put-down, and there is little chance of getting their positive power. A second way to ensure that your criticisms protect your recipient's self-esteem is to make sure you avoid phrasing a criticism as a right/wrong issue. It's too much pressure to be right all the time, yet I've met few people who like to be told they are wrong. Furthermore, with true criticism—because it is only your evaluation—there is no right or wrong. An editor's criticism of a manuscript is not right; it is simply her evaluation. But if the editor makes her position right, she is making the author's wrong. Self-esteem will be attacked, and the results will probably not be positive.

You can also protect the person's self-esteem by remembering to allow your recipient to save face (which is not possible if you make criticism a right/wrong issue). Using phrases such as "Perhaps you are not aware of this" (even if you think he or she is aware) or "This is one way to do it; perhaps there are some other ways to explore" will do the trick.

Recall the opening examples. The advertising director's criticism would more likely be effective if communicated in these terms: "How about spacing the pictures out and using some brighter colors?" The manager would be more likely to help his sales trainee improve if he said, "You might find it more effective if you periodically ask your prospect if she has any questions. This will keep her involved."

Besides allowing you to get through to your recipient, criticism that protects the self-esteem has other benefits. One is that it paves the way for future criticism. Since the recipient's ego has been left intact, or even enhanced, her perception of you is likely to improve to the point where she sees you as a credible source, someone whose opinions deserve to be considered carefully. Consequently, later criticisms are welcomed, even sought. This of course allows you to help develop the individual over time. Another benefit of criticism that takes the ego into account is that it improves the quality of the relationship. Your conscious effort not to attack or wound communicates that you appreciate and value the person. The recipient's sense of this helps you both build and maintain a supportive relationship that is characterized by trust. In effect, protecting self-esteem helps ensure that you will get the power of positive criticism.

Tip #5:

Choose the Right Words

You can always choose the words that come out of your mouth. And it is best if you do because the words you use to criticize often dictate whether or not the power of positive criticism will be realized.

For example, the words a manager uses when criticizing one of his staff can either make her listen or not. Your words tell her how you are feeling, what you think, and what she can expect to happen to her. When you begin a criticism, your assistant is usually thinking along these lines: "Am I in trouble?" "Will I lose my job?" "How important is this?" Everything you say is interpreted by the recipient in the context of her needs, hopes, and concerns about her job. Make sure you say what you mean.

Many times, slightly altering the words you use makes a great difference. Criticizing your assistant by saying, "Your work is below our standards" will probably evoke a more defensive response than "Your work is not quite up to our standards." The first statement declares that the assistant is doing poor work, while the second statement (with the appropriate voice inflection) suggests she is close to doing satisfactory work.

If you are the boss, your words become authoritative and carry extra weight. Even if your staff member refutes your criticism, you can still back up your words with action. You may, for instance, tell your staff member, "Your work is way below our standards." She might think or say, "You're wrong." Wrong or right, however, you have work power; you can act on your criticism and fire her or take some other punitive action. When you are the boss, what you say *does* matter.

One way you can begin to use the right words is simply to avoid emotionally loaded negative words. Using the power of positive criticism is based on getting your recipient to be receptive to you. Using emotionally loaded negative words reduces receptivity. Your assistant may be rash, but telling her that she's impulsive and careless, or doesn't think things through, is not going to awaken her receptivity. Your coworker might have acted ineptly at a presentation, but calling him an idiot is not the track to take. Emotionally loaded words have the effect of blaming and shaming the recipient and threaten the self-esteem, too. Destructive labels help no one, and using them is a sure way to miss the power of positive criticism.

It is also good policy to pay attention to the words and phrases you use when initiating a criticism. One guideline or technique that I've noticed to be particularly effective, especially with those who you might expect to be defensive, is expression of positive criticism intent. Positive intent statements are formulated by thinking about the ultimate positive goal you want your criticism to accomplish. Positive criticism intent statements emphasize the task to get done.

For example, an author reports that his editor began her criticism of her manuscript by saying, "Well, my goal is to make this the best book possible. Here's how I think that can be done. . . ." The author went on to say that as soon as he heard his editor's intent, "it put me in the mood to listen to her thoughts. After all, my goal was the same as hers: to make it the best book possible."

Statements of positive criticism intent are effective for many reasons, but chief among them is that they immediately communicate to the recipient that the criticism has a positive goal. At the same time, the statement helps the recipient focus on the task of the criticism (to make this book better). Focusing on the task of the criticism, rather than the individual, is important because it depersonalizes the criticism, thus making it less likely that the recipient will fall into a defensive posture. In short, positive criticism intent statements help both parties in the criticism encounter to remember one of the basic functions of criticism: to make things better.

I have also found it a good practice to avoid using the words "always" and "never." These words, especially when coupled with accusatory "you" statements are like aiming a shotgun at somebody. "Always" and "never" are gross generalizations, and, like fault-finding "you" statements, are sure to ignite defensiveness. The rule here is "Never say always or never." A more choice word is "sometimes." "Sometimes, your work needs to be more thorough" will go a lot further in achieving positive results than "You work always needs to be more thorough." "Sometimes" is usually true; rarely is "always" or "never" true.

Another word that creates havoc for criticism is "should." "You should have done it this way" is frequently part of the criticisms we give and receive. The problem is, when you tell a person what he "should have done," you are implying that what he did was wrong. Defensiveness surfaces and you will most likely hear the response, "I couldn't." What word do I prefer instead of "should?" Try using the word "could": "Next time you have to deal with this customer, you could. . . ."

Using the word "could" helps your criticism perform one of its important functions: It creates options for the recipient. Rather than implying that what the person did was wrong, your criticism is simply providing different approaches for the task at hand that the recipient may want to try. Also, by using the word "could" you communicate to the recipient that you are not rigidly set in your views, which is implied by the word "should."

These are only some of the examples of how little words and phrases can make a big difference; there are many others, too. Your lesson here is simply to recognize that when you criticize, you can choose the words that come out of your mouth; and if you do, you increase the chances that you will get the power of positive criticism.

Tip #6:

Criticize Your Criticisms

Here's a sex difference when it comes to taking criticism: Men are much more likely to reject a criticism that is valid whereas women are much more likely to accept criticism that is invalid. I don't know which is worse—rejecting criticism when it is true or accepting it when it is false. Either way, the implication for both sexes is that the criticisms you receive must be evaluated.

Just because criticism can provide you with valuable information for improving yourself and the work that you produce does not mean that you must act on every criticism given to you. After all, it might not be valid; it might not be in your best interest.

On the other hand, just because a particular criticism evokes your emotions does not mean that you should quickly dismiss it, which is exactly what happens when you get defensive. After all, if you thought about it, the criticism might be very helpful to you.

This last point underscores the meaning of appraising the validity of criticism: evaluating it to determine if responding to the criticism is in your best interest. It means collecting information so that your response is based on coherent thoughts rather than distorted emotional thinking. When you can appraise the validly of criticism, you increase your chances of finding the positive power in the criticisms you receive.

Although there are many things to think about that help

you determine the validity of criticism, I have found five par-
ticulars to be extremely helpful.

The first is the content of the criticism. Ask yourself,
"How important is this information?" A salesman may be
criticized by his supervisor for having a messy desk on the
grounds that it gives customers a bad impression. However,
if the salesman performs his selling over the phone, he will
probably not be motivated to clean house despite the legiti-
macy of the criticism. On the other hand, if his position
changes to one in which his clients are coming into his office,
the criticism will probably become more valid.

Your ability to appraise the importance of a specific criticism will be facilitated when you take into account the other
criteria. What you should remember is that the importance
of the criticism is not fixed; rather, it varies depending on
your own needs, the needs of others, and the context in
which it is given.

A second particular to consider is the source of the criticism. It's natural to be irritated when you believe the person
criticizing you doesn't know what she is talking about (when
we get defensive, we think just that). Be a little more rational;
focus on the criticizer's qualifications. Is she qualified to criticize you? How do you know? Remember that just because
you like somebody doesn't mean she is qualified to criticize
your work. Similarly, your negative feelings toward a client
or coworker are not sufficient to invalidate what he has to
say.

Although the source is qualified, you may still disagree.
Perhaps you are using different criteria, or maybe your critic
does not understand your goals. And for sure, the source of
your criticism has his own motives and agendas. Considering
all these factors will help you get a good idea on how much
credence to give your critic.

A third specific to take into account is the emotional context of the situation. To be sure, emotions affect how we give
and take criticism. When we are angry or hurt, we often say

things that we wouldn't if not for our emotional state. Most of the time, when the emotional context is one of distress, the criticisms have swelled out of proportion. Sometimes they are just outrageously invalid. These are criticisms that you need to let slide because responding with your own distress-filled remarks only worsens the situation.

On the other hand, if the emotional climate of the situation and the mood of the critic seem to be calm and solemn, take your critic seriously.

Your best bet is to be sensitive to the emotional climate when you are being criticized; remember that although the criticism might be emotionally exaggerated, perhaps it still has some validity.

How many people give you the same criticism? This is another good point to pay attention to because it will help you decide whether the criticism is a function of your behavior or if it has arisen out of a particular situation. For instance, a client criticizes you for continually missing your deadlines. You realize you have received this same criticism for other clients. To get the power of positive criticism, you would have to change your behavior so that you can change your results. However, if you note that your work is timely for other clients, then perhaps it behooves you to investigate why you are having trouble meeting the deadlines of this particular client. It might be that the deadlines are unrealistic, or it might be that the project is more difficult than you anticipated; you might also find it boring. The point is that when criticism is consistent, focus on changing yourself. When it is inconsistent, examine the issues that make the criticism unique to the critic and/or situation.

Assessing the fifth criterion requires you to do a cost analysis: You need to figure out how much energy this is going to cost you and what benefits you can expect. Of course, your decision as to whether or not it's too much energy will be directly related to what you see as the potential benefits. If you can see few or no benefits from action on a specific criticism, then surely any energy expended would be too much.

It is difficult to judge the potential benefits of a change unless we are prepared to accept the criticism constructively. Being aware of the benefits change may offer is in itself an incentive to positive action and a source of energy. But many times, recognizing these advantages often depends on how the criticism is communicated.

Therefore, don't assume your critic will tell you the benefits or offer you an incentive. To do an accurate cost analysis, ask your critic, "What will I gain?" Ask your question in a concerned rather than a hostile manner: "I'm interested in knowing how doing what you suggest will help me," or "Can you share with me how you think this will affect us?" A response like this helps each of you learn the other's motives. Furthermore, by focusing on positives rather than negatives, you will be making the criticism improvement-oriented.

Sometimes your critic will not have any clear benefits in mind; when this happens, it usually dawns on him that perhaps his criticism isn't valid. Other times, he will be able to explain to you many benefits that will motivate you to resolve the criticism. In effect, you're looking to see when you will receive a significant return on your investment of time and energy.

A final point to remember is that when you appraise the validity of criticism, use these five appraisal criteria together. Each of them—content, source, emotional context, consistency of criticism, and energy required versus benefits— interacts with the others. For example, trivial criticism may take on great significance if it comes from your boss or most important client instead of a coworker or subordinate.

Here is an effective four-step methodology to help you put this tip into action:

1. Select a criticism that you recently received and write it out in detail.

2. Rate the criticism according to each criterion on a scale of 1 to 9, with 9 indicating that it's in your best interest to change.
3. Look at your evaluation to help you determine the validity of the criticism.
4. Do this procedure several times to help you internalize it.

What is most important to understand, though, is that by internalizing this tip, you slow your appraisal system down, thereby increasing your ability to think nondefensively. Instead of quickly dismissing a criticism for defensive reasons, you begin to withhold your reaction until you have scanned it to see how it fits with the aforementioned criteria. In effect, even if it is for just a moment, you constructively reflect on what is being said. You come to evaluate the criticism on its own merit and, by doing so, increase your chances to get its positive power.

Tip #7:

Involve Your Recipient

Getting your recipient involved in the criticism process is important for many reasons but mostly because having him interact with you in a positive manner greatly enhances the chances for productive resolution. Each of you begins to contribute to the task. A synergy begins to build.

There are many ways to get your recipient involved in the criticism process. You may, for example, have your assistant problem-solve the criticism situation with you rather than simply providing instructions on what to do. You can also get your recipient involved in the criticism process by having him report back to you periodically concerning progress.

One of the more important ways of keeping your recipient involved is asking for his input about what you are saying. This action serves multiple purposes. For one, it keeps your recipient involved at the moment. Your request will force him to pay attention and contribute to a dialogue. Second, asking for his thoughts will help you determine whether your recipient understands your message; if not, it will be impossible for him to respond productively.

Many times when we criticize, we fail to assess whether the recipient understands. We make an unstated assumption that the recipient comprehends the message. Often we are mistaken; then we get angry when the expected results do not appear.

Besides clarifying understanding of the issues and creating dialogue, asking for the recipient's input will also provide you with his views on the situation and a sense of whether he agrees with your criticism. If there is a disagreement, find out why. Many times, his reasons for disagreeing will supply you with insights that will change the status of your criticism. Although you can force the person to agree if you are the boss, there is little probability that he will attack change with enthusiasm and commitment. Knowing that he disagrees permits you to pursue a different avenue or to reassess the validity of your criticism.

You will also find that when you ask for the other's input, you will minimize her defensiveness. Most of the time when we are criticized, we are thinking of our rebuttals even before the critic is finished. We can hardly wait to respond and frequently interrupt to defend ourselves. When you let someone know you want her feedback, her receptivity increases because she knows that she will get the opportunity to express her viewpoint.

A good way to build this point into your criticism is to use the prediction technique. You implement this gambit by saying something like, "This is how I see things; I know that you may see things differently, and that's okay, or you may agree."

If in fact the recipient appraises the situation differently, you have already given permission and said it is okay to disagree. You guide the recipient into thinking: "He's right. I do disagree. I'm glad he can accept that. But let me listen to what he says." In essence, your statement makes room for your recipient's point of view, and this makes the encounter more comfortable. If in fact he agrees, then you are already going in the same direction.

Why is this called the prediction technique? Because your recipient is going to either agree or disagree with you regardless of what you say. Since we know that most people are mentally disagreeing with the critic as he speaks, it becomes a smart strategy to overtly acknowledge that the recipient is "allowed" to disagree because he can do it anyway, and because most people become more receptive when they know they can freely express their own opposing views. The point is, whether your recipient agrees or disagrees, the criticism process is facilitated.

Another way to keep your recipient involved in the criticism process is for you, the critic, to become more involved in the task of helping your recipient make the changes necessary for the criticism to be resolved. Use a co-op plan.

To do so, you must sit down with the recipient of your criticism and together formulate a plan that will help the individual respond productively to the criticism. It is usually successful because it lets the individual know that she is not alone in the change process. You keep her involved by involving yourself. You will find the co-op plan to be especially useful for criticized behaviors that take time to remedy.

Consider the case of the computer programmer who was considered very talented but a pain in the neck. He would demean the intelligence of others, criticize their every comment, and talk to people as if they were computers. It was no wonder that his team members usually forgot to inform him when meetings were being held; as you would expect, the team was not performing up to its capabilities.

To reprogram the programmer, the supervisor helped him change his alienating behaviors by meeting with him and developing a plan; together, they wrote out a series of goals. The programmer would, for instance, forever substitute the word "customer" or "client" for "user" (the idea was to get him to view himself as a businessperson supplying a service to customers rather than as a programmer interfacing with a user). He also agreed to "ask more and tell less" at meetings so he could get the design information he needed. He agreed to be more polite.

Although implementing the plan wasn't easy, his supervisor recalled that "the upshot was that over a period of time, he definitively improved to the point where he had changed his perceptions of internal clients. Complaints fell off and co-operation increased."

The supervisor was effective because instead of putting the responsibility of change solely on the subordinate, the superior increased his involvement in the criticism process by helping the subordinate develop a concrete—and ultimately effective—plan to resolve the criticism. In effect, the supervisor's increased involvement "forced" the programmer to stay involved and resolve the criticisms.

To be effective, make sure your co-op plan covers the following six points:

1. Emphasize the importance of the person's job. A person who believes her work is valuable is likely to respond in a positive way. Make sure you state why her job is important; otherwise, you will be giving a pep talk.
2. Seek out her evaluation of the behavior or situation you are criticizing. This shows that you respect her opinions and that you expect her to take part in resolving the criticism. It also indicates that your own ideas are not fixed and that you are willing to learn from others. She is likely to respond with explanations and suggestions for improvement rather than with denials or excuses.
3. State clearly how resolving the criticism will benefit her.
4. Enlist the subordinate's aid. The new plan of action must make sense to the individual if she is to be motivated by it and committed to it. Ask the individual how the criticism can be dealt with, then involve her in formulating the specific implementation of that plan.
5. Ask her how you can help her implement the plan and how you can be supportive. This is the most important part of the co-op plan because it directly in-

volves you in the implementation of the change process. It drives home to the individual the point that you are going to cooperate in and share the responsibility for the change process.
6. To get the power of positive criticism, do your share of the plan and help the individual do hers.

If you fail to get your recipient involved, you will find yourself not only giving a laborious monologue but also facing the Herculean task of trying to help another person improve her behavior without her assistance.

On the other hand, getting your recipient involved in the criticism process is most important because it helps you and your recipient make criticism a cooperative process, which lays the groundwork for good relationships, greater commitment to resolving the criticism, and a common reason for generating a meaningful solution. All of these factors help you get the power of positive criticism.

Tip #8:

Remember the Merits . . .
Without the "But"

Can you remember the last time you heard positives when you were criticized? Think about the last time you gave criticism; did you mention any positives?

Criticism is an evaluation of both merits and demerits, but the fact is that most people omit the merits when giving criticism, something you cannot do if you want to realize the power of positive criticism.

You may be one of those who believes that including some positives when you criticize is a simple way to soften the blow. To some extent, you are right. But there are several more important benefits of including the merits that help make criticism productive.

One is that it brings into awareness what the person is doing right, something we often forget when we are angry or disappointed and giving a barrage of criticism. Being aware of a person's merits, whether you express them or not, allows you to perceive the person in a more positive manner. This keeps anger and disappointment in check. When you explicitly state the positives, it conveys that you're aware of and appreciate his efforts. The recipient's self-esteem is intact, if not enhanced.

A few specifics about the nature of your positives. First, your positives must be sincere. Giving a soft-soap job is likely to make matters worse—if you can't come up with any positives, don't invent them. Also, it's essential that the positives you are mentioning are important to the recipient. You may think that telling your secretary her letters are typed neatly is a positive, but this may be something she takes for granted. For her, a positive may be, "I liked the way you worked that last line and gave it a personal touch."

Now we come to a very important point: Be aware of when in the criticism session you give the positives. The most common sequence is to begin by telling the person all the good things he is doing and then catalog what is wrong. I have found this approach to be ineffective. Why? Examine the sentence structure that typically accompanies this type of presentation. It looks like this:

State the positives————BUT————state what is wrong.

If you recall the last time someone criticized you using this format, you will recognize its problems. When someone starts by giving you the positives of what you are doing, the typical reaction is to think, "What did I do wrong? Here comes the ax." You start to anticipate the negatives to come and begin to plan your rebuttal prematurely. And, let's not forget that the expectation that negatives will soon come forth elicits negative emotions. Defensive behavior is brewing, and you can forget about the power of positive criticism.

One reason for this cognitive response pattern is that people are not used to getting positives in a work situation. When they do, these positives are usually followed by negatives. That is just what happens here. You hear the word "but," and your expectation that the negative is coming is confirmed. The next time is sure to be the same.

Now the other problem with this method of criticism: The word "but" is a negation. Semantically, it tells your recipient to forget about what she has just heard—the positives.

She then hears the negative part of the message and is apt to leave the encounter with feelings of failure. Even if the positives were well deserved and meant sincerely, you have inadvertently diminished their impact. And your recipient is likely to forget that you even mentioned them. She leaves thinking that you have put her down, even if that was not your intent.

Let me give you an alternative method of giving the merits so that they are heard and remembered. Instead of starting with the positives, start by focusing on how the person can improve; then conclude by telling the person what he is already doing well. The formula looks like this:

State how the recipient can improve————AND———— state the positive things the recipient is already doing.

This format capitalizes on three points. The first is that most people respond positively when you tell them to make something better. Recall in Tip #3 that self-esteem theorists believe it is a natural tendency to want to develop oneself. When you tell a person how he can do something better, you are tapping into this tendency, and your recipient becomes more eager to hear your pointers. This is obviously a good way of making your criticism improvement-oriented (Tip #3).

Second, this format takes advantage of the fact that people are much more likely to act productively on the criticisms they receive when they feel good. When you end your criticism on the upbeat, you are getting the recipient to experience positive affect, and this good-feeling state translates into motivational energy.

The third point involves the word "and." Whereas the word "but" semantically negates its previous message, the word "and" does just the opposite: It integrates the preceding statements. Instead of thinking "I'm a failure," your recipient is more likely to think, "I am doing a lot of good things, and I can be that much better if I improve on some others."

Although use of the word "and" rather than "but" is subtle, its long-term effects are powerful. In the end, it helps your recipient realize it's okay not to be perfect; she does some things well and can improve on others, and this is pretty good. The acceptance of this notion is a sign of healthy self-esteem and a token of positive criticism.

Tip #9:

Tell Them What You Want

There are many reasons most criticisms fail to get the job done, but one of the most common is that the critic does not tell her recipient what she wants to have happen; she does not give a solution or option on how to handle the task. The recipient then tries, with good intent, his own solutions, which far too often are not what the critic had in mind.

Seeing no change, the critic becomes frustrated, angry, and destructively critical of the recipient. From the recipient's point of view, this is unfair. After all, he is making a concentrated effort to resolve the criticism. "Why try if this is what I get for my efforts?" becomes his attitude. He begins to feel that the burden of change is solely on his shoulders.

Getting no help and seeing little positive effect from his efforts, he begins to feel impotent, his self-esteem is diminished, and the criticism remains unresolved. The result is that everybody loses. This sorry state of affairs can be avoided if the critic offers a solution as part of her criticism.

What is the solution to the criticism? It is simply how you think the criticism can be resolved. It is your answer to improving the situation. The obvious reason for providing this to your recipient is to give him a clear direction for improvement. Telling your subordinate "You need to be more of a team player" may be improvement-oriented but is still not as effective as saying, "You can improve your peer relationships by not canceling meetings with them at the last minute, getting your share of the work to them on time, and

verbally being supportive of their efforts." You are suggesting specific actions to take; you are teaching appropriate
skills and knowledge.

Besides giving a clear message of what you want and
what you expect, offering solutions is important because it
demonstrates your helping spirit. Your recipient sees that
you have taken the time and energy to think about how he
can become a better worker. He sees that your intent is to
help rather than put him down. You become an ally instead
of an enemy. You are showing your recipient that he is not
alone, that you will share the responsibility for resolving the
criticism. When this message is communicated, it converts
criticism into a mutual problem-solving process, one that is
cooperative. Change becomes easier when you have a partner
(recall Tip #7).

Many people, especially managers and supervisors, balk
at offering the solution, on the grounds that their recipient
should be able to generate the solution himself. "It's his job;
I shouldn't have to do it for him" is the attitude. If you follow
this thought, you need to remember the principle of response
generalization—teach people how to respond in situation A
and when situation B comes along, they will come up with a
similar response modified to the new situation. Applied here,
recognize that you are teaching him an example of what con-
stitutes an effective response, instead of thinking that you are
doing your subordinate's job.

For example, if you tell a saleswoman that she needs to
improve the way she waits on customers, she will want to
know how. Telling her "It's your job to know how" will be
of little help. However, instructing her to accompany customers to the dressing room not only gives her a specific action
to take but also helps her understand what the concept of
attentive service is all about. The chance increases that when
she later sees a customer who has purchased several items
leaving the store, she will spontaneously approach her and
ask her if she needs assistance with her packages, then thank

her for her business and invite her to return. To reiterate, offering a specific solution helps you teach appropriate skills and knowledge in a general sense.

What about the times when you don't know the solution? Acknowledge this and add, "If we put our heads together, we can figure it out." Usually, you get the power of positive criticism.

Tip #10:

Be Timing-Oriented

A manager wanted to criticize two subordinates for being too competitive with each other. Their lack of cooperation was resulting in frequent power struggles that led to costly project delays. He planned his criticism and took them both to lunch at a local Chinese restaurant. Before the waiter took their order, the manager subtly remarked, "Well, I like everything. You two decide what to get." This prompted a short discussion and the dishes were mutually selected. After all was happily consumed, the manager remarked: "I really enjoyed that. You guys did a good job in ordering; everything went well together. And when we get back to the office, I will expect the two of you to cooperate in the same manner." And so they did.

Is this an example of making criticism timing-oriented? You bet it is! The manager was smart enough to choose an environment that he could use to heighten the recipients' receptivity to his criticism. And to make it doubly effective, he structured a task for them to do that illustrated how he wanted them to interact with each other—cooperatively.

To get the power of positive criticism, you must remember that there is a time and a place for every endeavor. Criticism is no exception. Critical remarks that otherwise might be offered and accepted in a positive way can be rendered ineffective—not because of their content or how they are said but because of when and where they are made, because of the recipient's state of mind at the time and the critic's own mood, too.

Perhaps there is no bigger truth in getting the power of positive criticism than to say that your sense of timing is crucial for getting the results you want. Consequently, it is good policy whenever you criticize to be alert to the time, the place, the presence or absence of other people, and the psychological state of the criticized person.

But when is the best time to criticize? Answer some questions and find out. Do you criticize someone in public or in private? Your initial thought might be, "Private, of course." After all, a boss's well-put criticism of a subordinate at a group meeting may be rebuffed because the subordinate feels embarrassed and thinks she has to defend herself in front of her peers. Or, she may nod her head in agreement but internally be focusing on what her coworkers are thinking about as she is being criticized. These points make a good case for the boss to select a private time with his subordinate to deliver his criticism.

But it may also be that the best time to criticize the subordinate *is* at a staff meeting, in front of her peers. Consider the boss who strategically criticizes her subordinate in front of her peers because she anticipates that her reaction will be less argumentative than if she did it privately. She believes that her subordinate's past behavior reflects a strong need to impress her peers by being open to criticism and that the group atmosphere will pressure her into thinking about the criticism.

You are the head surgeon in an operation, with three of your residents assisting. You see one is mishandling a procedure that could have dire effects for the patient. What are you going to do? Criticize him after the patient dies so you can do it alone?

It's a staff meeting where the goal is to go over an ad layout. The copy is off, although the colors, type, and photographs are perfect. When does the copywriter get his criticism?

Now, is better to criticize privately or publicly?

Next question. How long should you wait to give criticism? You would be in the majority if you thought "Right away," but I will give you one exception to that practice: Never ever criticize someone when you are angry. Not because you may say things with emotional exaggeration, but because social psychologists have shown that when criticism is perceived as being motivated by anger, it is discredited; the criticism is thought to be motivated by anger and is not what you really think. Simplified, your criticism loses impact and credibility when others think you are speaking out of anger.

Similarly, never ever criticize others when they are angry. As an emotional reaction, anger causes physiological changes in your brain that have the effect of making you more rigid in your thinking; you are locked into your perspective. If the recipient is angry, you know he is rigid in his thinking and will probably respond with "I don't want to hear about it." What he means to say is that "I can't accurately listen to what you are saying." In the case of anger—yours or the recipient's—you are best to hold your criticism until there is some calmness.

A writer living on the West Coast told me that he had some criticism to give his editor about how she was handling the promotion of his book. Although he wanted to tell her right away, he waited several weeks. He thought his criticism would be more positive if he timed it with a face-to-face meeting.

Instead of criticizing a sales rep immediately after his presentation for not leaving enough time for questions, the sales manager delivers his criticism just a few minutes before the rep's next presentation with a "Remember to leave enough time for questions."

Now, how long should you wait until you deliver your criticism?

How, then, do you use timing to give you the power of positive criticism? Obviously, there are no rules as to when and where to criticize. What must be developed is the awareness and skill of using environmental, situational, and psychological factors to increase the recipient's receptivity to your criticism.

For application, before you deliver your criticisms, get in the habit of asking yourself, "Is this the best time to criticize this person? Is it necessary to do it now? Would I want to be criticized in this setting? Is she in the right frame of mind? Am I in the right frame of mind?" Your answers will help you become timing-oriented, which will make it a lot easier for you to get the power of positive criticism.

Tip #11:

Use Questions Socratically

An editor for a large metropolitan newspaper reported a great example of using questions Socratically. His story goes that he was supervising a journalism student who had high hopes of bettering Lois Lane. She was to spend a semester in the city newsroom with the expectations of gaining an understanding of the inner workings of a major newspaper and (of equal importance) developing the ability to report, organize, and write a news story worthy of publication.

The city editor had a reputation of being very tough, and it was well known that his sarcastic, critical comments often left his best reporters feeling undeserving of a byline. Nevertheless, he was considered an excellent newsman and was committed to developing this budding cub reporter.

To do so, he would give her weekly assignments, one being that he would present her with the facts of a news event that she would then have to structure in an orderly journalistic manner.

A deadline was set for each assignment; the editor would follow standard procedure. He would read the article, scribble his criticisms where needed, and get a rewrite with the expectation that it would not only be better but that her next new assignment would show improvement, too. After several assignments, the editor stated his assessment of his student: "She writes well. Her organization stinks."

Because he had been spending a good deal of time reading her stories and writing down his remarks, he was also becoming a little frustrated that her work had not shown the improvement he demanded. Also, he recounted that during the several times he criticized her work directly by telling her exactly what to do and how to do it, she had become argumentative. He was getting tired of her defensive behavior coupled with her lack of improvement.

The situation came to a head one afternoon when she presented him with her latest story concerning the vandalism of a local school. Reading it on the spot, the editor saw that once again she had poorly organized the facts. In his language, it stunk.

His eyewitness account of what happened next is as follows: "I was about to jump all over her. But before I did, I caught myself. I realized that putting her down was not going to help. And telling her what to do did not seem to be effective either. I tried a different approach. I remember it going like this":

Editor:	Hey, did you hear about that murder?
Reporter:	What murder?
Editor:	The one that came in on the wire service.
Reporter:	Who got murdered?
Editor:	Jack Smith.
Reporter:	Where did it happen?
Editor:	At his house.
Reporter:	When did it happen?
Editor:	This morning.
Reporter:	How did it happen?
Editor:	He got shot.
Reporter:	Why?
Editor:	You just asked the six most important questions in newspaper writing: what, who, where, when, how, and why. Go re-

> write this and put that information in your
> lead!

"She smiled and ran back to her desk to make the changes;
from then on, her work showed the organization I wanted."

Kudos to the editor. Like Socrates criticizing his student
Plato, the editor used questioning as a means of stimulating
the recipient to generate her own answers. In this case, by
asking one strategic question, the editor spurred the reporter
to ask a series of questions; these questioning responses provided the information that the editor wanted the reporter to
highlight. His interaction with the reporter stimulated her
thinking and protected her self-esteem; consequently, she not
only felt good about making her work better but was excited
to do it. In effect, criticism by question leads your recipients
to discover solutions for themselves.

Don't lose sight of this last point. When people come up
with their own solution, their self-esteem is enhanced because it satisfies their competency need—a desire to feel competent and master their environment. By coming up with the
solution, the recipients gain a sense of competency. An
added benefit is that since the recipients generated their own
solution, they are more likely to be committed to following
through on the needed actions. You will find criticism
through questions to be especially effective with individuals
who typically respond to criticism with defensiveness.

Here's the four-step procedure for using questions Socratically:

1. Devise a question or series of questions whose answers lead the recipient to the crucial information:
   "How do you think the sales division will react to
   your marketing report?" rather than "You should
   have checked with the sales division for their reaction."
2. Do not ask questions in a condescending manner, a

manner that implies "See if you can guess the answer." Try "What if" phrasing: "What if you were to change the target test market?"

3. If the recipient comes up with an unexpected answer, explore it. If not satisfied, state your views as another possibility: "This may be true. It may also be that. . . ."

4. If you feel as though you may appear to be manipulative or playing games, be straight and openly implement criticism by question: "Let me ask you a few questions; then I will share my thoughts, and we can come up with some answers together."

A closing thought—perhaps a warning—is to remember that if you turn a question mark on its side, it becomes a hook. Too often, we ask critical questions that may be hooking the other person into defensive behavior. For example:

"Where did you get these sloppy data from?"
"From Jack. I thought . . ."
"You should have asked me before you asked Jack."

Such questions are hooks because you know in advance that regardless of what the recipient says, the answer will not be acceptable. Instead of profiting from the exchange, the recipient experiences a sense of helplessness, failure, and loss of self-esteem. If you can remember not to use questions as hooks but rather as an artful method of criticism, you will unquestionably increase your chance to get the power of positive criticism.

Tip #12:

When Words Don't Work, Use Your Actions

A psychiatric head nurse at a Veterans' Administration hospital explained her criticism situation:

> It's very important that each day staff members record their therapeutic sessions on the patients' charts so the evening staff knows what happened on the day shift. Rarely is the staff negligent about the procedure. One exception was a psychology intern. He had a habit of sometimes leaving work before he made his progress notes. The first few times this happened, I mentioned it, reiterating the importance of the procedure. He agreed and said that he would make sure it didn't happen again. But it did. In fact, it happened on a regular basis. Every time he was criticized, he agreed and said it wouldn't happen again. But his behavior never changed.

Almost every manager and supervisor can relate to some derivation of the above. An employee is continually criticized for behavior and continually agrees to change—but doesn't. In effect, your verbal criticism, no matter how clever and creative, is ineffective. It is quite frustrating.

In these situations—when the criticized behavior continues despite your repetitive verbal criticisms—I suggest you communicate in a behavioral manner, that is, do something rather than say something.

Most of us think of giving criticism as something we *say* to another. Behavioral interventions expand this thought. They require you to think of giving criticism as anything you can do—not just say—that helps a person improve. They are based on the premise that criticism is an interaction with both parties influencing each other. Thus, if you change your behavior, it sometimes forces the other person to change how she responds to you or to the situation.

The head nurse described how she managed this common criticism situation with the intern:

> Finally, I decided that talking to him was not going to help so I had better do something else. I came up with a plan. I knew he left the hospital about 3:30 every day. So, at about 2:45, I went down to his office with one of my coworkers and said, "Could you please come up and do your progress notes?" We did this every day for two and a half weeks. A couple of times, he said he'd be up in a minute, but rather than risk his not coming, we said we'd wait for him. One day at 2:40, as we were about to go and get him, he walked into the nursing office and said, "I thought I would save you the trip." From that day on, he'd always come to the nursing office at 2:30 to make his progress notes. We changed his behavior by changing ours.

Here are four steps to devising your own behavioral intervention when your words don't work:

1. Pinpoint the criticisms you give repeatedly and to no avail.
2. Decide on an intervening behavior that may force

change by requiring the recipient to develop a new behavioral response: Literally spend five minutes a day with your assistant checking to see if she has put files back where they belong; call your subordinate daily to remind him to keep his coworkers informed of his schedule; give your subordinate a nonverbal signal (scratching your head) every time he interrupts a coworker in a meeting.

3. Be consistent with your intervention.
4. If the problem continues, devise a second behavioral intervention.

If you can remember that sometimes the way to give criticism is to change your behavior as a means for helping others, you will be more apt to experience the power of positive criticism.

Tip #13:

Use Your Expectations

Sometimes we expect that a person is going to continue the behavior that we criticize; we do not think she is going to change. In this case, our expectation may cause us to give premature criticism—as soon as the person approximates the behavior in question, we criticize.

Take the superior who expects that his staff member will once again be late with his work. As the deadline approaches, the boss will point out to his subordinate that once again he has failed to meet his deadline. However, the deadline has not actually arrived; in fact, the subordinate can still meet it. The boss has become overly critical of the subordinate and, at the same time, has communicated through his premature criticism that he doesn't trust him to succeed. This message is internalized by the subordinate as, "I can't do it. Why try?"

The irony is that this premature criticism undermines the subordinate's true efforts to improve and causes him to do exactly what the superior wishes to avoid—continue missing his deadlines.

Expectations: They are the mental bets we make with ourselves about the outcome of events, our behavior, and the behavior of others. They often reflect our goals and standards. Our expectations are powerful forces in the criticism process. In the above example, you can see one way expectations affect how you give criticism.

But expectations also impact how you receive criticism. Take the case of your next performance appraisal. What are your expectations of what your manager is going to tell you? You may internally be expressing negative expectations by thinking, "This is going to be terrible. I'm not going to be able to handle this. I'm really going to get angry. The guy really wants to nail me to the wall."

By having these expectations, you lower your ability to handle the criticisms effectively. The first sign of negativity from your criticizer becomes a confirmation that your expectations were "correct"—"See, I was right. This guy is putting me down." The expected anger now comes your way. In effect, your negative expectations trigger your defensiveness.

Expectations impact criticism in other ways, too. Many times, criticism comes out of unmet expectations that were never communicated. Other times, criticism is based on unrealistically high expectations—no matter what the result, it isn't good to be good enough.

Expectations: It's impossible not to have them. Since they are potent forces in impacting your results, it is to your advantage to know how to make expectations work for you. Consider the manager who knows how to use positive expectations to build a team's confidence. He can be assured that his team's chance for success increases. The subordinate who knows how to change his boss's expectations from "I don't expect my subordinate to criticize me" to "I expect my subordinate to criticize me" is going to have a better relationship with his boss and thus increase his chance for success. And those of us who can use our expectations to make taking criticism a more productive process are going to profit.

My years as a "critiqueologist" have given me some general guidelines that help make the relationship between criticism and expectations a positive one, so I want to pass them on to you. There are three steps, all easy to apply.

The first is to become aware of your expectations by identifying them. I suggest you write down what you expect from yourself, your boss, your coworkers, and other significant people in your work life. This may seem laborious, but once you write down your expectations, you will be able to appraise them more accurately and thus prevent yourself from giving criticism that is motivated by unrealistic expectations.

Your second step is to examine whether your expectations are steeped in reality. There are several ways to tune in to the reality of your expectations. One is to use similar past experiences as your baseline. If you expect your sales staff to increase their sales by 30 percent over the next year but past experience shows the best you've ever done is a 20 percent increase, you are probably setting setting the stage for some unwarranted criticism of your staff. Realistically, a 15 percent increase would be terrific, and 10 percent would still be great. By using past experiences as a database, you have a valid method for forming a realistic evaluation of how your staff is performing. Simply compare your expectations to your past performance, and you will get a pretty good idea of whether or not your current expectations are realistic.

It is good policy to ask others what they think. Sometimes it's difficult to be objective because of personal biases and emotions. Sharing expectations you have of yourself or others with other people gives you input as to whether or not you are being too hard or easy on yourself or on others. They can help you evaluate your expectations in terms of reality. This is often a good way to become aware of the negative self-criticism you might be delivering; it is also a good method to help you identify when your expectations of others are exceedingly high.

Furthermore, you can assess whether or not your expectations are realistic by assigning percentages to your expected outcomes. Quantifying the chance (60 percent chance, 30 percent chance, 10 percent chance) helps you think clearly about whether you really believe the expectation is going to be met. Once you assign a percentage to your expectation, you can modify it as the situation evolves and, in the process, develop a realistic outlook. This brings up an important point: Expectations will serve you best when they are elastic rather than static.

Making expectations realistic does not mean you should not set them high. The perennial track star, a best-selling author, and a movie star all have exceedingly high expectations for themselves—as do their coach, publisher, and producer. Yet their past behavior dictates that these expectations are realistic. But for the average high school track athlete, the first-time author, and the fledgling movie actor, the same expectations would be unrealistic, to say the least.

Step three for making your expectations work for you is to communicate and clarify them to those who are involved in your work activities. Letting people know what you expect of them provides them with important information—what you think and what your needs are. It also provides them with the opportunity to determine if your expectations are realistic and if they believe they can perform to your expected level. If they think they can't, they are able to explain their viewpoint, and together you can reach a realistic perspective.

Expectations: Since they are part of the working day, it is good business to make them work for you, especially if you expect to get the power of positive criticism.

Tip #14:

Acknowledge That It's Subjective

If you ever had anyone respond to your criticism with a "That's your opinion," I hope you acknowledged that point. Criticism is your opinion; even if it is based on objective fact, it is still your subjective evaluation that is responsible for judging the importance of, for example, a particular attribute or behavior.

Yet, consider some daily criticisms that are usually given verbatim: "Your work needs to be improved," "You need to get along better with your peers," "You're not doing as well as you should be." All of these criticisms are presented as facts, when in truth their content is a matter of judgment. Others might judge the same behavior differently.

All too often, many people forget that the criticisms they give are their personal evaluation of the situation. They lose sight of the fact that their own perceptions are usually quite different from those of the person they are criticizing. In fact, it would be quite naive for you to think that others will interpret an event the same way you do. Yet, this is an underlying thought for those who deliver your criticism as an irrevocable fact. Furthermore, these people interpret any opposition as defensiveness. In truth, the recipient is not getting defensive; he, like the giver, is simply giving his own evaluation of the situation.

The most common way people transfer their subjective evaluation into an objective fact is through "you" messages—statements that you are doing or not doing something. "You" messages almost always provoke defensiveness because they evoke the finger of blame. They imply, "You are at fault for causing this problem," "You should have known better," "You are bad." Most of the time, blame is unnecessary because people seldom do poor work on purpose; their behavior is usually motivated by a desire to meet their own needs and is not intentionally aimed at making your work harder.

Thus, you are much more likely to get the power of positive criticism if you remember to acknowledge that your criticism is subjective, not a black-and-white objective fact. When you acknowledge that your criticism is subjective and that it is your own individual perception, you remove the notion that the recipient is definitely doing what you claim or needs to do what you say. Instead, it arouses his curiosity as to why you think as you do—you are inviting the recipient to compare his assessment with your perception. You are communicating that there is room for his views. Not feeling as though you are saying he is wrong or blaming him for a particular action, he becomes more at ease and begins to make a concentrated effort to capture your point. Instead of inciting an argument filled with accusations, you are able to initiate a constructive dialogue.

Furthermore, when you mentally note that what you say may be true only for yourself, you are much more likely to search for the right words, eliminating broad generalizations and statements of blame.

What makes it difficult to acknowledge that criticism is subjective? Sometimes, it is because you forget an important point about cognitive appraisal—different people can interpret the same event differently. Awareness of this point will help you remember that your criticism is subjective and help you make allowances for the differing perceptions of others.

On a practical level, you can increase your awareness of this point by prefacing your criticisms with an "I think" statement. But doing so presents another difficulty—it's called risk.

Sharing your thoughts in the workplace, especially with a boss or client, can sometimes be a scary experience. We are afraid that an idea might be disparaged or a thought might reveal our lack of knowledge. Yet, this is what is required when you give criticism: You must disclose your thoughts about how you are evaluating a particular situation/behavior/person, etc. As you put your thoughts on the table, you become vulnerable because your thoughts are now subject to being evaluated by others. How many times have you been at a meeting and when the boss asks, "Any ideas?" you keep quiet, even though your mind is filled with ideas? Although not productive, it is certainly safer to keep your thoughts to yourself; disclosing your ideas allows those ideas to be criticized.

It is not my intent to tell you to self-disclose all of your criticisms; that could be politically unwise. The point for you to capture is that to give positive criticism, you have to be willing to take a risk—that risk is to have your own thoughts evaluated by others.

I've noted over the years that productive criticizers deal with this quandary by strategically assessing the pros and cons of verbalizing their thoughts versus keeping them to themselves. Unfortunately, you really don't know if your assessment is accurate until after the fact. But one thing is for certain: If you are not willing to put yourself on the line, there is very little chance that you will experience the power of positive criticism.

Tip #15:

Put Motivation in Your Criticisms

One of criticism's primary functions is "to motivate to do better," so it is safe to assume that for your criticisms to have positive power, they better be motivational to your recipients.

Motivation is an age-old psychology concept, and there are numerous ways to define it. For our purposes, motivation refers to "anything that arouses one to pursue a particular course of action," ranging from being thirsty (which will make you seek water) to the possibility of a raise (which may incite you to make more sales calls). Motivation comes in all shapes and forms: thoughts, feelings, a particular word or two, a tangible object, a nontangible need.

Whatever shape it takes, though, the goal of motivation is to rouse you to action. Indeed, your criticism may be improvement-oriented and packed with invaluable information, but if the criticism lacks motivation, don't be surprised if your recipient, even with good intentions, doesn't act on it.

Assess your own criticisms for motivation. Do you find your subordinates or staff members react to your criticisms as though they *have* to do better, or do you find that your criticisms have the impact of making them *want* to do better? Do you find that your criticisms get improvement results for only the short run, or do you find that the impact of your criticisms initiates a long-term desire to improve?

If your recipients want to improve after your criticisms and their work continues to improve, then you are probably pretty good at putting motivation into your criticisms. If you experience the opposite, then it is probably time to start putting motivation into your criticisms.

Broadly speaking, at its best putting motivation into your criticism is constructing and delivering the criticism so that the recipient's response is marked by a *wanting* to improve rather than a feeling of *having* to improve. In other words, putting motivation into the criticism has the effect of getting the person to want to do her best, not simply to do or to settle for what is good enough.

On a concrete level, putting motivation into your criticism is explicitly showing the recipient how he will benefit from taking action. Since each criticism situation is different, the place to start is by tuning in to your motivational assumptions for the individual in question.

Whether you are aware of it or not, your motivational assumptions, beliefs, and attitudes about your recipient strongly influence how you deliver your criticism. Take the common scenario of the subordinate who is consistently late with his work. How would you motivate him to improve his performance?

If you are a manager or supervisor from the school that says people are motivated by either the carrot or the stick, your delivery of the criticism is apt to sound like this: "To get that promotion, you will have to meet your deadlines." The motivational assumption is that the individual wants the raise and that the criticism, delivered as such, will prompt him to achieve the desired results.

Now, a second manager follows the school of thought that proposes people are motivated to act when they perceive their actions will help them meet their specific, nontangible psychological needs. Her criticism will be more along these lines: "People will really appreciate you if you can get your work in on time." The motivational assumption of being appreciated by coworkers is important to the individual and will thus influence him to act in a way that will help him meet that need.

Which is the best track to take? Which is right? Obviously, either approach could be effective, depending on the individual and the situation. The key point is, in either case, your motivational assumptions influence how you give criticism.

Most individuals are usually not aware of their motivational assumptions and thus do not see the connection between them and how they give criticism. This seems to be true even when their criticisms are ineffective.

Besides not getting the desired results, these critics inevitably feel frustrated, angry, and helpless. In the end, they say, "The guy's a real problem. I've spoken to him a dozen times, and he doesn't change." The truth is, it is the critic who perpetuates the problem by not changing her motivational assumptions, which forces her to use the same ineffective incentive over and over. No wonder the behavior stays the same.

In contrast, those who are able to consistently use the power of positive criticism are aware of their motivational assumptions. This grants them the critical factor of *motivational flexibility*. If they see that one incentive fails to motivate, they switch to another motivational assumption and incorporate different incentives into their criticisms. Their chances for success multiply exponentially.

In the example of the first manager, his second attempt to criticize might sound like the second manager's first attempt, and vice versa for the second manager. Both of them would be acting on the premise that since the first incentive didn't work, try another one. And if their second approach is also ineffective, they will search for a third way, using a different motivational tactic.

The easiest way to become aware of your motivational theory and assumptions is to think about them. Ask yourself if your motivational assumptions are getting the results you want. If not, you may want to question them. Once you become aware of your motivational assumptions pertaining to a specific individual, you can identify specific incentives that may rouse him to action.

Most executives, managers, and supervisors state that they do build incentives into the criticisms they give, but what they fail to recognize is that, all too often, the incentive offered is important only to them. They misperceive the value of the incentive to their recipient. Trying to get a subordinate to change because it will increase your own chances for being successful is apt to have little effect. Pointing out to a coworker that you both stand a chance of having even more responsibility if she meets her deadline will have little motivational effect if she doesn't want more responsibility, to say nothing of the effect if she actually wants less responsibility.

For criticism to be an effective catalyst for change, there must be a payoff for the recipient. He must clearly see how he will benefit. He needs to know, "What's in it for me?" Offered an incentive he values, he thinks, "Hey, this is for me! I'm doing this for myself."

To identify incentives that may put motivation into your criticisms, focus on those around you and ask yourself what you think motivates them, what is important to them. Your answers will give you ideas about what turns them on.

Observe their behavior; if your relationship permits, ask them what motivates them. Their answers will give you valuable insights into their inner workings that may come in handy at a later time.

Most importantly, it is excellent policy to get into the habit of asking yourself, before you criticize an individual: "How will this motivate the individual to improve?" Your answer will increase your awareness of the motivational assumptions and help you identify what might be the right incentive at the right time.

Once you have selected the incentive, build it into the

criticism you give by explicitly stating it to your recipient. If it is not effective, don't get frustrated and blame the recipient. Simply practice motivational flexibility. Inevitably, you will find the right incentive, and with it, you will also find the power of positive criticism.

Tip #16:

Use Their World

An administrator in a university biology department complained to me that one of her assistants was having difficulty getting along with the researchers, who in this particular university were well-known names in the field. In gathering information, I learned that the assistant was slow in getting paperwork to the researchers, argued continually with them, and frequently ignored their requests to recruit experimental subjects.

The assistant saw it differently. She contended that the researchers were a pain in the neck—they constantly made demands, gave little thanks, and were arrogant to boot.

The administrator confirmed that her assistant's perceptions were in fact quite accurate. Nevertheless, the way she interacted with the researchers was unprofessional and unacceptable.

The administrator had intervened several times in constructive ways. She had arranged structured meetings to discuss the problem. She had asked the assistant what she thought could be done to make things better and had asked what she could do to help. She had explained the importance of getting along with the researchers. She had even used an occasional threat—all to no avail.

After listening to the administrator's complaint, I asked, "What does the assistant like? Does she have a hobby? What is important to her?"

A few days later, when the time was appropriate, the

administrator spoke to her assistant once again: "You know, these researchers are very special. They are just like your plants and flowers. They need a lot of care. They have to be watered daily and given some sunshine, and you need to talk to them. When you do that, they will bloom and become stronger and prettier. And it will be easier for you to take care of them." By the end of the following week, the administrator noticed that her assistant's attitude and behavior toward the researchers had improved markedly.

What the administrator said might sound hokey and contrived, but the fact is, it helped her finally get the results she wanted. She used a metaphor to get into her assistant's world—she talked about the researchers in a manner that enabled the assistant to relate to them in a familiar and enjoyable way. This is exactly why metaphors are effective tools for giving criticism.

Does this mean that you should always make the recipient "the captain of the ship"? Of course not. But there are many times when you will find metaphor to be a handy tool to help you get the power of positive criticism. One case is when your criticism is not effective because it is not meaningful to the recipient and thus does not motivate him to change, even when you have tried linking the change to monetary or other incentives.

Here, you may find that your savior is giving criticism through metaphor backed by the psychological principle that metaphor serves as a gateway to a person's subconscious. What this means is that metaphors allow you to enter the recipient's world in a way that is meaningful to him. Put another way, you are putting "your picture in his frame." The criticism now taps in to the recipient's motivational system—it has become meaningful and thus motivates action.

A second calling for the use of metaphor arises when your criticism is either hypersensitive or sure to evoke defensiveness. Here, criticism through metaphor is helpful because it allows you to present the information in a more benign manner. You may find, for example, that your subordinate is too impulsive on his projects. Yet, every time you broach the subject, he responds with defensiveness. It is also a well-known fact that this subordinate spends his vacation time on fishing trips. Your criticism might be more powerful if you told him, "This project is like going after Jaws. Go slowly, wait until you are sure that you have it, and then carefully reel it in."

A third situation in which you might find criticism through metaphor to your liking is when you have to criticize a group—whether it is a team, a department, or a division. Crucial to this use is choosing a metaphor that applies to the whole group, a unifying metaphor so to speak.

Case in point is the medical director of a hospital who criticized all of her department heads for not working as a team; they were overly competitive with each other and more interested in the welfare and reputation of their particular department than the welfare of the general hospital.

After analyzing the situation, the medical director concluded that directly confronting the issue—"Cardiac department, why are you not working with Rehab?" or "Radiology department, what is going on with Surgery?"—would elicit anger, blame, and defensiveness, hardly the stuff she wants in a hospital environment.

Instead, she sought to change her staff's behavior by giving them the information in the form of a metaphor that she knew her entire staff would relate to; she used the metaphor of a human body. She explained in all-too-familiar terms what they already knew—what happens when one organ fails to work in conjunction with the system. Almost instantly, the physicians got the point. "Things got better," she told me.

Two general guidelines to use this tip effectively are:

1. Choose the right metaphor. Listen to those around you talk; know their values and their interests. Don't

use a sports metaphor if your recipient isn't a sports fan.

2. Do your homework to familiarize yourself with the special language of the metaphor. If you don't, your recipient will realize you don't know what you are talking about.

Metaphor is a rich and revealing way of communicating, and being able to use metaphors is one of the most important skills for unleashing the power of positive criticism.

Tip #17:

Follow Up, Follow Up, Follow Up

Every once in a while, you skillfully present your criticism and it is productively acted upon. Other times, you skillfully present your criticism, your recipient is eager to change, but the change is short-lived.

After getting you the reports on time for a month, your assistant seems to go back to her pattern of being a few days late. Your boss becomes a better listener after you have spoken to him, but the next week he is back to his abrasive, autocratic style. Your team responds to your criticism by scheduling more meetings, but six months later, the meetings are sparse again. In short, the power of positive criticism is temporary.

Despite the fact that you have given effective criticism and your recipient is motivated to respond, you still have to make sure she keeps on track. Put another way, if you want the power of criticism to be permanent, you would do best to always remember to follow up.

In its strictest sense, following up means that you observe whether your recipient is responding as agreed upon and that you directly communicate your observations to the recipient. More to the point, though, follow-up means recognizing that criticism is a developmental process. Change is not necessarily easy; in the case of criticism, you are often trying to get your recipient to develop a different way of responding. Following up helps you accomplish this task.

On a practical level, if you perceive that your recipient is not responding as agreed upon, share your perceptions with him. The same is true if you observe that improvement is occurring. In both cases, your response not only lets your recipient know your perceptions but also keeps him aware that you are still involved and intend to see the criticism resolved, as agreed upon.

Many critics commit two fouls when following up. The first is assuming that if they observe no improvement, the recipient is not committed and is ignoring their criticism. They then begin destructively criticizing the recipient or, just as badly, record their observations and save them for the annual performance appraisal. They forget that developing new habits or improving behavior is very difficult and usually does not happen overnight. An accountant might be able to clean up her bookkeeping procedure in a week, but it might take a teacher six months to improve his rapport with his students.

The second common error is noting improvement but failing to acknowledge it, often focusing on the fact that the recipient is still not performing up to the established standards. Again, change does not happen overnight. If you fail to acknowledge positive progress, no matter how slight it is, the odds are good that your recipient will revert to her old ways because she sees that her efforts are bringing her no rewards, not even a positive stroke. Since change is hard, especially with no incentive at hand, it's easy for those old habits to reemerge. Besides, if you wait until your recipient is perfect at her task, you will be waiting forever.

Here is how you can implement your follow-up: As soon as you see progress, speak directly to the person. Your acknowledgment will act as positive reinforcement and will keep the recipient's momentum going, enabling him to do even better.

If you see your recipient is having difficulty in taking productive action, reacknowledge the criticism and ask how you can help. Most of the time, we tell the recipient to try harder, which may or may not be effective but, in either case, puts the responsibility of change on the recipient. Asking how you, the critic, can help directly involves you in the process and becomes a built-in follow-up system—as long as you are helping, you are following up. For example, the principal who sits down on a weekly basis to help the teacher revise her criticized lesson plans is following up in a much more productive manner than the principal who merely asks every week how things are coming.

Perhaps most important is that following up on your criticism demonstrates to your recipient that your initial expressions of wanting to help were more than just a pep talk. He begins to believe and feel that you are committed to helping him and inevitably begins to look forward to your criticisms because he starts to view them as part of a mutual effort to further his career and as information that will help him grow. In other words, following up helps your recipient to see the power of positive criticism.

Tip #18:

Know Your Criteria for Criticizing

Two experts in the field of criticism, Aristotle and Plato, advocated that a good critic bases his opinions on a specific criterion. I would have to agree and I am sure you would, too. Indeed, you would be a rare manager if you never had any debate over what is a good performer, what is a good organization, what is a good manager, etc. Similarly, you would be a rare employee if you did not, on several occasions, question the criteria used to evaluate your worth or, for that matter, even understand the criteria that were being used.

The concept of having criteria—reference points for judgment—is an integral part of criticism because it underlies your rationale for formulating your evaluation. Your criticism of a marketing report, for example, is influenced by how you think a marketing report should be presented. Your criticism of your assistant's dealings with your clients is no doubt a reflection of how you think she could conduct herself. In both cases, your criteria influence your decision of what is good and what is bad. Furthermore, your criteria, especially in the context of performance evaluation, become responsible for important decisions.

There are all sorts of issues around the concept of criteria. I will give you a few to think about, but you and your staff will have to think about the implications and work out the details. I'll use an example that is familiar to me.

Many times, I start out a criticism seminar by asking participants to jot down the most important criteria they will be using to evaluate their forthcoming experience. Pooling the participants, I hear:

"Is it practical?"
"Can I use it immediately?"
"Did it hold my interest?"
"Was he a good presenter?"
"Did I learn anything new?"
"Is he as good as Martin Luther King, Jr.?"
"Did it meet my needs?"
"Was he funny?"
"Did I learn three specific things that I can use?"
"Did he keep me up?"

I ask the group, "Which is the most important one?" There is much discussion. I ask the group, "Is it fair for me to be evaluated by these different criteria? I might meet your needs, but I might not make you laugh. I might be a good presenter, but I'll never have the speaking charisma of Martin Luther King." There is more discussion around the equity of criteria and how to handle using multiple criteria.

In the end, there is little resolution, but the class does pick up on the tip of identifying your criteria in advance. Doing so helps you in multiple ways.

First, you immediately recognize that your criteria are subjective: They are what you think are important. They clarify your standards and your values, what you think is good and what you think is bad. Those who use other criteria are sure to disagree. In fact, using different criteria for evaluating performance is a major source of conflict in many organizations. On this point, it is smart to also be aware of the criteria that others are using.

Identifying your criteria in advance also helps make criticism much more focused and accurate because you have a specific reference point in mind that you are trying to get the recipient to achieve or reach. This latter point implies that it is not enough to identify your criteria; you must also communicate them to those you expect to criticize.

Do not confuse communicating criteria with the tip of communicating expectations (see Tip #9). Criteria have to do with your measuring standards; expectations communicate what you want to happen. Telling your subordinate that his criterion for success is a 20 percent sales level communicates the criterion you are using to make your evaluation. But it might also be that you expect him to do better than the expected criterion. You can see how this expectation—if not recognized—can complicate the final evaluation you give him.

There are many ways to communicate your criteria; speaking about them is probably the most common, but it is not always the most effective. Sometimes, your best bet will be to show the criteria. A book editor, for example, told me that every time she had to work with a new author, she would send him a copy of a book that, in her mind, demonstrated the writing style of a quality management book. She "showed" her criteria, and the new author reported how helpful this was to him.

Identifying your criteria before you criticize is also important because it forces you to remember that criticism makes sense only in the context of your criteria. Criticizing a saleswoman for doing a poor job normally makes no sense if she doubles her quota. However, if your criterion for being a good saleswoman is having happy customers and this particular saleswoman has customers who feel as though she took advantage of them, then your criticism is valid. A principal who criticizes the most well-liked teacher for being poor at his job may seem out of line, but not if his criterion is how well the teacher's students do on reading tests rather than the teacher's popularity.

To apply this tip effectively, before you criticize (whether for customer service, peer relationships, or the cleaning of your office), ask yourself:

◊ What criteria am I using? Do they reflect the behavior I am criticizing?
◊ Should I be using additional criteria?
◊ Are others aware of the criteria I am using to judge their actions and results?
◊ Are my criteria fixed, or do I change them with the times?
◊ What do others think of my choice of criteria?

Your answers will pay off in the way they help you shape and communicate your criticisms into more effective evaluations, an important criterion that contributes to getting the power of positive criticism.

Tip #19:

Listen to Yourself

One of the many ways that our thoughts influence how we feel and behave is through the things we say to ourselves. These internal conversations are the mechanisms that allow us to bring to consciousness the appraisals we make and the expectations we have. The statements we make to ourselves precede, accompany, or follow the things we feel and are directly linked to them. If you believe that criticism is negative, then it is a sure thing that when you are being criticized, you are talking negatively to yourself.

"This is worse than I thought," "When will he be finished?" "He's going to fire me next"—statements that probably sound familiar to you—are common statements that people say to themselves when they are being criticized. Not only do these self-statements reflect your negative concept of criticism, but more to the point, they make it impossible for you to be receptive to what is being said. In fact, your self-statements are making the situation much worse. To counteract this negative trend, you must develop the skill of listening to yourself.

Being able to listen to yourself will allow you to monitor exactly what you are saying to yourself when you are criticized (and when you are giving criticism). As you become better and better at listening to yourself, you will be able to pay better attention to your self-statements. You can then examine your thoughts to see if they are helping you or hurting you. With this awareness, you can begin to modify them to help you become more receptive to the criticisms you receive. In effect, you will be using your self-statements as instructions that will guide you through the criticism process.

A good way to practice this tip is to set aside five minutes a day in a quiet environment and to sit back and listen to the internal conversation that is currently going on in your mind. Pay attention to how fast your thoughts are and whether you talk in the first or third person. Imagine yourself to be listening to someone else's phone conversation. Your goal is to familiarize yourself with how you talk to yourself.

Listening a few minutes each day for at least a week will be a tremendous boost to your skill in hearing yourself talk. You will soon note that in many situations—while playing sports, listening to your partner, standing in line at a movie— you are paying attention to your internal thoughts. This awareness is what allows you to use your thoughts productively.

Once you have become used to hearing yourself, you can begin to focus on what you say to yourself when someone criticizes you. Chances are, you will find that your internal conversations at such times are filled with destructive messages that not only make the situation worse but also are not true.

These statements—those that you hear yourself saying when you are being criticized—will tend to be habitual; how you talk to yourself when your boss is criticizing you on Monday is apt to be the same as when he criticizes you on Friday.

Inevitably, because of the frequent replaying of the tape, your thoughts (when you are criticized) come more and more quickly, until they seem to occur without any prior reasoning or reflection. They have become automatic thoughts.

Your automatic thoughts usually have the following characteristics:

◊ They are often irrational. Surely an employee who is told that her work needs to improve and thinks "I'm a failure" is being irrational.

◊ They are almost always believed by you. Even though many automatic thoughts are irrational, you usually accept them as true. Rarely do you tend to evaluate or challenge them.

◊ They usually are brief in form. A rising executive may say "Zip" to tell himself that he will not get another top assignment.

◊ Your automatic thoughts tend to accumulate, acting as cues for other thoughts. One depressing thought may trigger a whole chain of depressing thoughts. (Here is an example of an automatic thought that typically arises when a boss criticizes a subordinate. Automatic thought: Blew it. Really means: I screwed up this assignment. My boss thinks I'm stupid. There goes my promotion. What will my family say? They will leave me.)

The problem is that these thoughts occur in a split second; because they seem to be automatic, we rarely take the time to acknowledge their destructive content. Instead, we quickly become defensive about the criticism.

When you can listen to how you talk to yourself, you will be able to pick up the counterproductive thoughts that you have early in the criticism process and use them as a cue: You need to talk to yourself differently, in a way that helps you listen to the criticism and to be more receptive.

I recommend the technique of counterpunching. It is based on the idea that your counterproductive critical thoughts are mental punches that you inflict on yourself. Inevitably you become senseless. Like the boxer, you need to fight back; you need to counterpunch by matching every counterproductive statement you make when you are being criticized or about to be criticized with a rational comeback, a statement that helps you keep things in perspective so that you are able to act in a more productive manner. For example, if you hear yourself saying, "He's out to get me," counterpunch by saying, "How do I really know that? He's just telling me how to do better." If you catch yourself saying, "I'm a failure," counterpunch with, "Just because I didn't do something well doesn't mean I am a failure. I will learn so I can do it better." Your counterpunching will allow you to eliminate the destructive messages that you hear when you are criticized and free you to hear the criticism with a more open mind so that you can decide rationally whether it is valid.

A good way to train yourself in counterpunching is to write down the destructive statements that you hear yourself making when you are criticized. Next to each one, prepare a counterpunch statement that you can use if need be. Knowing your counterpunches in advance will make it easier to talk to yourself rationally, even when the critic is destructive.

Similarly, for those situations in which you know you are likely to be criticized, write down several instructional self-statements that tell you how to act productively:

◊ Stick to the issues.
◊ Listen to what he says.
◊ I can learn from this situation.
◊ Take a deep breath and sit back.

Using self-statements like these is effective because they control your emotional arousal, guide your behavior in productive directions, prevent you from getting sidetracked, and give you confidence that you can cope with the criticism. In short, learning to listen to yourself helps you hear the power of positive criticism.

Tip #20:

Stay Cool, Calm, and Collected

Your heart beats faster, you breathe more quickly, your blood pressure is zooming, and you are apt to perspire. If you are exercising, you probably would welcome these physical responses as a sign of a good workout. Your system is on track, and you are on your way to getting in shape. But if you're giving or taking criticism, they are a sure sign that you're probably about to get bent out of shape and derail yourself from the track of success.

For many of us, criticism evokes strong emotions, particularly anger, when we receive it and and anxiety when we give it. These emotions—fueled by negative self-statements—intensify and speed up our physical arousal system to the point that it becomes disruptive to our thinking.

If your arousal is not checked, you lose your mental agility. If you are the recipient, you automatically lock out the criticism. If you are the giver, you become rigid in your views, convinced that you are right, and forceful in your delivery.

In either case, not being able to stay relaxed when you are giving or taking criticism will prevent you from staying focused when the heat is on. This is when criticism turns ugly.

On the other hand, if you can stay cool and calm during

the criticism encounter, you will be able to deal with the situation more effectively because you will prevent your emotions, in the form of defensiveness, from getting the best of you. Instead, you will be able to appraise the situation accurately and respond appropriately.

There are several actions for you to take that will help you stay cool and calm when you are either giving or taking criticism. The first is to become sensitive to the physiological responses that tell you you are becoming unsettled. You will be able to use these responses as a cue, a warning that your emotions are beginning to get out of hand. You can then make a conscious intervention to calm yourself, thus allowing yourself to evaluate the criticism for what it's worth. If you are the giver, your emotional arousal will tell you if you are too angry or anxious to give the criticism.

You can begin to learn how to use your emotions as a cue that things might be getting out of hand by monitoring your physical arousal level in a variety of situations. For example, monitor yourself when you are resting, reading a book, exercising, rushing to get to work, or being criticized. Focus on your breathing rate and heart rate, and get a feel for how they differ in different situations. You will soon note that your physical arousal system is much slower at rest than when you are in a rush or becoming angry. After a few days of monitoring, you will become very adept at noticing when your body is speeding up.

In a criticism situation, this physical sensitivity will pay off because it will enable you to quickly recognize that you are becoming aroused; this recognition will serve as a cue to calm yourself, perhaps by consciously breathing more slowly. You may also use your increased physical arousal as a signal that it's time to modify your self-statements, since your getting aroused probably means you are thinking counterproductively.

A second way to stay calm during the act of criticism is to develop a relaxation response, the ability to quickly calm yourself when you so desire, even in emotionally distressing situations. Your relaxation response helps you maintain a receptive attitude toward criticism because it keeps emotional arousal at a level that allows you to think rationally.

In a criticism situation, using a relaxation response will probably prevent you from getting angry or defensive. You remain mentally flexible and are able to evaluate as well as give the criticism more effectively.

To develop your relaxation response, first select a relaxation exercise to practice for ten days. One popular relaxation exercise to consider is the tense-relax procedure, which calls for you to tighten and relax the different muscle groups in your body. Start with your calf muscles and proceed to your thighs, stomach, shoulders, neck, and forehead. Tighten each muscle group for approximately thirty seconds and then release it. At the end of the exercise, your body will be in a state of physical relaxation. If this does not appeal to you, select another exercise. The key, however, is to practice the relaxation exercise within these four parameters:

1. Be in a quiet environment.
2. Be in a comfortable physical position.
3. Have the same mental image, key word, or key phrase in mind as you practice.
4. Have a passive attitude. Don't try to relax—let it happen.

After a few days of practicing relaxation, you may conclude that it doesn't work. You would be right. It takes ten to fourteen days to develop a relaxation response, just as it takes two weeks before you start to see the benefit of any exercise program.

Staying cool, calm, and collected during a criticism encounter isn't the easiest thing to do, but if you can do it, you will find the power of positive criticism to be quite relaxing.

Tips in Action

It's not as daunting a task as you think to apply the tips you need to get the power of positive criticism. To illustrate the ease of application, study the following "anatomy of a productive criticism," paying attention to how the criticism becomes more productive each time a tip is applied.

1. Your report is sloppy.
2. Your report needs to be improved.
3. I believe your data analysis could be more complete.
4. I would like you to include the Midwest projects in your data analysis.
5. I think the data analysis would be even better if you included the Midwest projects.
6. I think you will be in a better position to get your project approved if you include the Midwest projects in your data analysis of the situation because that will tell our clients that we have been successful on similar ventures. I am very impressed with your recommendations and analysis. I would imagine that you could do it in two or three days, and then we could go over it again. What do you think?

This last criticism is a far cry from the first. It applies many of the tips, such as:

◊ Tip #14: Using the subjective mode: "I think"; "I would imagine."
◊ Tip #8: Stating the merits: "Impressed with your recommendations and analysis."

◊ Tip #15: Giving the incentive: "Get your project approved."

◊ Tip #9: Offering a solution: "Include the Midwest projects in the data analysis."

◊ Tip #13: Setting a realistic time frame: "Two or three days."

◊ Tip #17: Planning follow-up: "We could go over it again."

◊ Tip #7: Involving your recipient: "What do you think?"

Although the final criticism would qualify as being positive, there are many other ways of communicating the same information to the recipient. For example, the final delivery might be, "I read the report, and I'm wondering if you think the Midwest projects should be included in the data analysis?" The semantics of this delivery take criticism to task by inviting the recipient to explore on her own the benefits of including additional information. It is a "softer" presentation in that it does not flatly state that you think the information should be included. In fact, the phrase "I'm wondering" implies that you are not sure of your position (even though you might be), thus increasing the chance that the recipient will not hear the criticism as pointing out a flaw in her work. This delivery also calls for a response; it prompts a dialogue. If the recipient responds by agreeing with you, you complete your task by choosing a time frame for the addition. If the recipient's response is along the lines of "No, I don't think so. Why do you?" or even a flat "No," you can proceed to mention some of the benefits of this addition, which you think will get the recipient to appraise the criticism positively. Note that in order to respond productively to the recipient's inquiry, you must be familiar with the same information that is contained in the first format (Tip #7 of the earlier list).

Which format is better? There are no specific guidelines except to consider whom you are criticizing, how he perceives you, and the history of your relationship. If the recipient tends to be defensive, the second delivery might be more effective. If the recipient holds you in high esteem, the first format would be better because it is more authoritative. It gives a concrete recommendation and specific reasons for change. If this is the first time you are criticizing the recipient, you may come up with a different delivery altogether.

In the end, it all comes down to knowing what you want to happen, thinking about how the recipient will respond, and figuring out how you can get him to respond productively. Doing so puts you on track for getting the power of positive criticism.

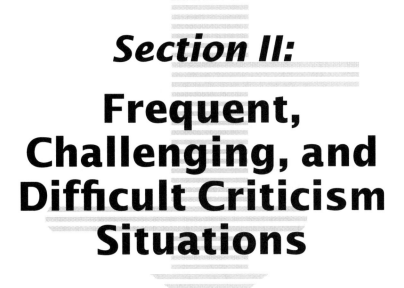

Section II:

Frequent, Challenging, and Difficult Criticism Situations

Over the last twenty years, I have listened to thousands of people, from CEOs to company chauffeurs, present their most difficult and challenging criticism situations. Thousands more have given me the same information through surveys and group interviews conducted at their organizations (which include the likes of AT&T, IBM, Hyatt, TRW, Hughes Aircraft, McDonald's, Intel, Avon, Bristol-Myers, Merck, 3M, Warner-Lambert, CIA, Secret Service, FBI, EPA, IRS, Department of Labor, PBS, and Young Presidents Organization), hospitals, school systems, and executive education and MBA programs (at Wharton, Cornell, UCLA, RPI, NYU, University of Washington, Penn State, and other leading business schools).

From these data, I have selected the fourteen criticism situations that are commonly cited as being frequently encountered as well as difficult and challenging to handle.

Sometimes, what makes the situation difficult is the nature of the relationship you have with your recipient.

Other times, it is difficult because of the specific behavior you wish to criticize. There are also those times when it is difficult because of how your recipient responds to you. Regardless of the reason, the common denominator in these situations is that criticism is difficult to give or take, let alone to be able to get its positive power.

In this section, I will provide you with proven-effective strategies, techniques, methods, and interventions to help you get the power of positive criticism in the most difficult and/or repetitive criticism situations you are likely to encounter.

To facilitate your learning, keep these four points in mind as you read each situation:

1. The goal of criticism in each situation is to *change* the situation for the better. Thus, each situation illustrates how to use criticism as a catalyst for change, one of its chief functions.
2. The techniques/interventions recommended are based on specific empirical research or on a well-accepted theory. In effect, the techniques and strategies show how to creatively and effectively apply all of the tips mentioned in Section I. Getting the power of positive criticism requires you to translate the tips into strategies and interventions that help you change a negative or potentially negative situation into a positive encounter with positive results.
3. Although the recommended techniques and strategies vary across situations, you will find that they have broad application; you will be more likely to get the power of positive criticism if you think of how they can be applied to your own unique situations.
4. Remember that there is no one right answer to any situation but rather several interventions that

could all be effective. Be sure to be thinking of how else you could handle the situations presented. The more you do this, the more likely it is that you will be able to get the power of positive criticism from your own most difficult and challenging criticism situations.

So You're Afraid to Criticize Your Boss?

The hands-down winner for the most difficult criticism encounter at work—whether it is a Fortune 500 company, small business, government organization, hospital, or just about any other work environment—is, "How do you criticize your boss?"

The solution, of course, varies across bosses and situations, but you will give yourself a head start if you rid yourself of the belief that if you criticize your boss, you will suffer negative repercussions. Indeed, this perception is what most working folks say is the major barrier to criticizing their boss.

While it is true that this scenario plays out occasionally, it is the exception. Most bosses—especially the most effective ones—welcome criticism from their subordinates. What they do not like is being embarrassed, threatened, or undermined. For criticism that is packed with these qualities, negative repercussions become the norm. Obviously, perhaps more than any other work criticism encounter, successfully criticizing your boss depends not only on what you say but how you say it.

For openers, adhere to three major ground rules. The first is to make sure your boss is receptive to being criticized. While there are no absolute ways to do this, you can use some of the softer signs suggestive of his attitude about being criticized. Does he openly solicit criticism and act upon those criticisms that are valid? Is he open to change—do you see policies and procedures that are flexible and dynamic—or are things basically kept the same? Is he accessible to you, or does it take a formal meeting to spend some time? And what about his visibility—is his office door shut to keep out his staff, or is his door kept open to invite drop-ins? If you think your boss has low receptivity to criticism, you might be politically wise to learn how to adapt to the situation rather than attempt to change him.

If you think your boss is receptive to criticism, your next rule is to make sure it is appropriate to voice it. Here, recognize that the power structure of your organization must be honored. In other words, make sure the boss you are criticizing is your boss or your immediate supervisor. To criticize a superior whom you do not directly report to could be career hurting. If you need your criticism to reach this person, your strategy is to use your own boss to carry your message upward.

If your immediate boss stonewalls your criticism, you can proceed to go over her head, but make sure you inform and invite: "Boss, I don't think we are making progress on this point. I am going to speak to Jane. Perhaps you would like to be there when I do." It's been my experience that such a statement usually evokes increased thoughtfulness about your point. If not, and your boss does attend your session with the next-higher authority, the senior superior can hear her comments and yours as to how the criticism can be resolved. It also gives the senior superior a chance to see how your boss responds to criticism.

Also make sure that you are criticizing your boss for something she is doing that affects your work; to criticize her for actions that do not impact your performance would be uncalled for; if you are not involved in the project, you cannot possibly know the details and motivation of the criticism.

For those situations in which you are not part of the project but the success of the project impacts your job, you will be able to still give your criticism, but only if you can demonstrate that the action your boss takes affects your job.

A sales rep for a cosmetic firm made use of this point when she criticized her boss's marketing plan for a new product. Although she had not been asked for her opinion, she approached her boss and said, "I read the new marketing plan, and I noticed that the product was going to be targeted to my territory. As you know, my major clients buy products that cost fifteen dollars or less. The product costs twenty-five dollars. Also, my clients tend to go for hand creams and basic shampoos rather than glamour products. So besides the money issue, I'm not quite sure that the need will be there. If you want me to try to market it, I'll do my best, but I'm not sure we will be successful." Her boss, after reviewing the demographics of the sales rep's territory, agreed with her and changed her marketing plan in reference to the target area. Note that although the sales rep disagreed with her boss's plan, she indicated she would still give it her best effort. It is important to communicate to your boss that you will still follow the course he sets to the best of your ability—even if you disagree.

if you are set to criticize your boss, make sure you know what you are talking about. Remember, in most cases, your boss does not expect you to criticize her. This is a tough expectation to combat; therefore, it is essential for you to remember to validate your criticism. Otherwise, your boss may not only dismiss it but may begin to see you in a negative light, which no doubt will affect your job and your future ability to criticize her. Some ways for you to validate your criticism include collecting and analyzing data (if available); accurately documenting how your boss's actions affect your work; and, if possible, consulting with other people.

The third rule for criticizing your boss is perhaps the most important: Avoid a power struggle. You must be careful that the way you present your criticism does not threaten your boss's self-esteem or his job security. If it does, your boss is apt to become defensive, and you can almost always count on the fact that once you and your boss lock horns, he will come out on top. The results for you are that your criticism is rejected and the status quo is maintained. Thus, any strategy for criticizing your boss must protect his self-esteem and acknowledge, implicitly or explicitly, that he is the superior.

With these ground rules in mind, I have found two techniques that have proved to be consistent winners for criticizing your boss. The first is to present your criticism to your boss in a way that emphasizes the validity of the criticism per se. The point here is not to present yourself as a valid source of criticism but to present your criticism as important and valid information. You are maximizing the significance of the information rather than taking the position that you, the subordinate, know best.

Instead of coming on as a know-it-all, you present yourself as sharing valuable data that relate to both your jobs. Your superior, instead of having to accept or reject a criticism, is now in the face-saving position of merely having to evaluate the information you are supplying. If the information is valid, there is an excellent chance your superior will take action. Some ways you can build up the validity of your criticism are: citing authoritative sources, submitting supportive data, and showing reference material to your superior.

A data analyst for a financial institution used this technique in criticizing her department head for the computer system she was considering. Instead of telling her boss that she was choosing the wrong system or that she knew which one she should buy, the data analyst gave her boss several current reports that indicated another system would be more responsive to their needs. Her boss, after reading the articles, changed her choice and thanked her subordinate for supplying her with "invaluable information."

A second recommendation for criticizing your boss is to phrase the criticism as a request for help after you have strategically (Tip #2) thought of the way your boss can help you by responding to your criticism.

Instead of pointing out what your boss is not doing right or what she needs to be doing, explain to her that you are having a problem and don't know how to solve it. Of course, from your perspective, the problem is your boss's behavior, but to express it as such will probably elicit your boss's defensiveness and create a power struggle that you will inevitably lose.

Therefore, express the criticism in the form of a "problem that I am having." The assumption is that your boss will recognize that the only way to help you is to change her own behavior. On the other hand, if your boss is able to help you solve the problem without changing her behavior, you still probably come out a winner because the situation has been changed for the better.

A secretary at an aerospace company used this technique with her boss, who had a habit of keeping her in the dark about his schedule. This made it difficult for her to set up appointments for him with his other subordinates and co-workers. Out of frustration, these people were continually pressing her to get them in to see her boss or at least to tell them when he was available. Her replying that she didn't know only intensified their anger. Furthermore, several times previously she had asked her boss for his daily schedule in advance and was rebuffed each time with "I will let you know my schedule when I want to."

At her wit's end, she approached her boss, stating that she had a problem and was wondering if he might be able to help her solve it. He became quite receptive, and she went on: "I don't know what to tell your coworkers and clients when they ask me when you are available. When I keep saying I don't know, they get frustrated and angry and take it out on me. I don't know how to handle it. Do you have any suggestions?"

After thinking about it, her boss replied that the only answer he could come up with was for him to let her know of his availability. However, he could let her know only two days in advance. The secretary acknowledged that even knowing his availability a day in advance would be helpful and thanked him for helping her solve her problem. Although this was not the perfect solution, it was a significant improvement over the previous situation. In effect, she changed her boss's behavior by getting him to "help" her.

As another example, suppose your superior is chronically late in providing you with the data you need to function effectively. You can say, "I'm having trouble running my department on those days when I don't have the weekly production figures. Can you give me some suggestions for improving this situation?" If your criticism is valid, chances are your superior will solve the problem—and resolve the criticism—by meeting her deadlines more promptly.

Those of you who take this approach can expect good results for a few reasons. The first is that people tend to be more receptive and responsive to information when they hear it as a request rather than a demand. Criticism presented as a demand usually threatens the recipient's self-esteem. It is as if the criticizer is saying that he is superior and that his concerns are more valid. Defensiveness comes into play.

When you phrase the criticism as a request for help, you communicate several messages that increase your boss's receptivity. First, you communicate that you respect your boss because you are asking instead of telling. As respect is communicated, your boss's receptivity is increased. Next, and more cunning, is that you increase your boss's self-esteem by voluntarily taking the "one-down position" of asking for help. You are implying that you can't do something on your own when you say outright that you need your boss's help. This is a put-up message that confirms to your superior that she is still superior. More important, there's a good chance that this ego boost will motivate your boss to take productive action.

Asking for help not only lets your superior know that she is needed, but that you, her subordinate, believe in her ability to achieve results. To phrase this more elaborately, when you explicitly ask your boss for help, you implicitly tap into her need to be needed and her need to achieve. For most people, satisfying these needs is a powerful incentive to action; when you arouse these needs, you are almost guaranteed that your boss will try to satisfy them by helping you generate a solution. Given these implicit messages, taking the one-down position requires self-restraint on your part, but the payoff is worth the price.

What about the impossible bosses? For such bosses, subordinates must create and develop different criticism strategies, trying each until one is successful. Some possible solutions: When a stoic boss doesn't tell you where you stand, bring up the organization's goals as a basis for determining specific criteria for next year's performance rating, so "together" you can monitor your performance accordingly. If the boss is a crisis maker, develop a strong network of relationships with coworkers that will help you get the information you need to decide whether each crisis is real or manufactured. When the boss is overcontrolling, work out of the office a lot if possible, exaggerate procedural obstacles, and frequently reassure the boss that you are on target. If the boss is truly impossible, if he has a short temper, or if he never listens, then attempt to offer criticism only if you can be clever and creative. Gear your strategy to answering the fundamental question: "How can I communicate this information so that my superior perceives it as useful?"

What is most important for you, the subordinate, to recognize is that the techniques for criticizing upward do not rely on direct, overt communication. The chain of command prohibits you from telling your superior that he's an idiot or that he made another foolish mistake, even if the superior says such things to you daily. Instead, to criticize upward and to create change at your superior's level, you must rely on informal relationships, timing, ambiguity, self-restraint, and implicit communication. Together, they give you and your boss the power of positive criticism.

The Wrath of Criticism

Anger. It is one of the most feared responses to criticism, even for the most skillful critics. And with good reason. Anger is a powerful emotion that, if not kept in check, can create trouble. Take the extreme example of the executive who criticized his staff member at a team meeting. The employee quickly got to his feet and hurled his coffee at his critic. He also sprayed a few innocent bystanders.

Studies have shown that people get angry up to ten times during the course of the working day, and your own experiences will tell you that many of those anger episodes revolve around the criticism process, especially giving criticism. Take the research that most individuals manage anger poorly, mix it with the frequency of giving criticism at work, and it becomes obvious why criticizing a person who responds with anger ranks high on any list of the most challenging criticism situations.

Why is anger such a difficult response to deal with? I've heard many reasons, but the common denominator, plain and simple, is that the anger response from others makes us uncomfortable. And all too often, we become angry, too.

True, the encounter is also difficult to deal with because the angry response from your recipient, especially if in a group setting, makes the atmosphere tense and embarrassing. Issues become sidetracked and communication shuts down. But these reasons are actually effects of the anger response as they enter into the picture only after the individual has responded with anger. The reason per se is that anger makes us uncomfortable.

This is not surprising considering the fact that anger is a

contagious emotion. If your recipient responds with anger, the chances are excellent that you will become angry, too. When this occurs, there is little or no chance that you will make your criticism positive; there is even less chance that your recipient will listen to what you say. In fact, he will probably point out that you are becoming angry and that when you calm down, he will be glad to speak with you. No doubt you will become even angrier.

Managing the angry response from others requires you to be able to use many skills simultaneously. The first is managing your own anger. Doing so allows you to overcome the discomfort of the experience so you can still conduct yourself appropriately. Some effective ways of doing this include practicing relaxation on a daily basis so that you can stay relaxed in the heat of the moment, using your self-statements as instructions to remind yourself to stay calm, and mentally rehearsing for the encounter by visualizing yourself handling it effectively. Once you can manage your own anger, you are more likely to be able to overcome the anger of others.

Here are some ways you can respond at the moment that will help you deal with the person who becomes angry in response to your criticism. You want to be able to keep your recipient calm. Calmness keeps her anger in check and also allows you to hold a rational conversation. As you speak, be perceptive; be on the lookout for her anger cues—voice rising, facial expressions, gestures. If you see them, stop speaking and invite her input. Since she is probably going to interrupt you anyway, asking for her input keeps it a dialogue rather than a soon-to-be argument.

When she does speak, ask her to speak slowly so you can really listen to what she is saying; at the same time, slowing her speech pattern will help her keep calm and avoid anger arousal.

At this point, you will probably hear a collection of denials, excuses, or accusations; these statements are generated by the recipient's angry state of mind, so do not make the mistake of debating them. Maintaining your calmness is crucial here; otherwise, you will be victimized by emotional contagion. Staying calm will let you do what you need to do: Hear what your recipient is saying.

Listening to anger is much more than sitting down, being patient, and letting the person blow off steam. Listening means making a concentrated effort to understand what the person is experiencing and why. Learning to listen is a skill that takes time and practice, but here are some specifics that will help you listen to the angry recipient:

◊ *Do not interrupt.* Interruption escalates a situation. It communicates that you are not listening. If you have the urge to interrupt, take a deep breath and remind yourself to listen.

◊ *Be aware of your body language.* Good eye contact and body posture are nonverbal signals that you are listening.

◊ *Summarize in your own words what you think the individual is saying.* Be sure to acknowledge his right to feel the way he does. Ask if you have captured the message.

◊ *If your recipient accuses you of not understanding, remain calm and express your desire to understand his views.*

◊ *Stay flexible.* Use what your recipient is saying to help you modify, dismiss, or persist in your criticism. By responding to what your recipient says, rather than simply reiterating your points, you will show your recipient that you are truly listening to what he says. This validates his feelings; his anger, at this point, is probably greatly diminished.

In effect, what these tactics allow you to do is to work through the recipient's anger so you can discuss the criticism in a productive dialogue. The better you are able to listen to your recipient, the calmer you will keep him and the more thoughtful he will become with regard to what you are saying.

If the angry response is persisting, you might find it effective to say something along these lines: "I respect your right to disagree with my thoughts, but I'm not quite sure why you are becoming angry." You can then offer your own thoughts: "Is it because you are feeling threatened? That is not my intent," or "Have I overstepped my boundaries?" Then wait for your recipient to answer.

In either case, I find the impact of such a response reduces your recipient's anger. It increases his awareness that he is angry, and this awareness helps him bring himself under control.

Many times, anger is a response to a threat so it is good policy to negate any irrational and defensive thoughts he is probably having. Something like "I hope you are not thinking that I am going to give you another assignment, or that I am no longer interested in your services, because that is not true; I just want to make things better next time" will usually do the job.

The above procedure is best applied when you are criticizing a person, and in the midst of that discussion, he becomes angry. Again, the idea is to manage the anger so that you can proceed to present and discuss the criticism at hand.

There are also those times when you know that at the first sign of being criticized, your recipient is going to become angry. For these situations, an effective way of minimizing your recipient's anger when you criticize her is to acknowledge at the start that you do not expect her to become angry or to compliment her in advance for not getting angry. For example: "I know you won't get angry when I tell you this" or "I appreciate your not getting angry when I tell you this. A lot of people would."

The rationale behind this strategy is that the initial statement is a self-esteem builder. If your recipient responds with anger, she loses the compliment. Most people choose to keep the compliment by managing their anger.

What about when you are the recipient of your boss's angry criticism? A secretary got tired of listening to her boss criticize her in an angry and abusive manner. He would incorporate insulting phrases into his criticisms of her work: "How could you be so stupid." "You spell like a high school dropout." "Sometimes I think you're deaf." (These were the mild insults!) She finally responded by writing down all his pet insults on an index card. The next time he began his tirade, she whipped out the card and said, "Here, Boss, I made it easy for you. Just go down the list." They both laughed, and the boss realized how inappropriate his behavior had been. He changed. While this is not a recommended tactic for every subordinate who is criticized by an angry boss, it does illustrate that there are many ways to handle a criticism situation.

To reiterate, there is no guaranteed way to keep a person from responding to criticism with anger. However, if you can manage your anger, keep your recipient calm, listen to what she is saying, and reduce her angry thoughts, then there is an excellent chance you can give your angry recipient the power of positive criticism.

It's Personal,
Not Business

"Have you ever had to criticize a person for personal hygiene?" The answer is a resounding yes for the majority of the working class. And although there is always a lot of snickering when the encounter is raised, there is no doubt that criticizing a worker for personal hygiene is a dirty business. Most people break out in a sweat at the thought of doing it. If you follow three steps, you still may perspire while giving the criticism, but what you say won't stink.

The first step is to focus on what makes it difficult to tell someone he smells. The most frequent response is that it is personal and not work-related. Yet, anyone who has worked with a person with poor hygiene knows that it is very difficult to work with someone who gives off offensive odors, whether it is a team member, boss, subordinate, or client. As to it being personal, it is. But so is all criticism.

Further exploration of the question inevitably leads to the root of the difficulty: It is embarrassing. In fact, most people find criticizing a person for personal hygiene to be more embarrassing than having to give any other type of criticism. Thus, the first step to handling the encounter productively requires managing the embarrassment of the situation.

To do this, you have to apply your emotional intelligence by remembering that all emotions (such as embarrassment, anger, and anxiety) provide us with valuable information that we can use to help navigate through life's encounters more productively.

Emotions are a complex interactive system of your thoughts, physical arousal, and behavior. Most people, when they criticize a person for personal hygiene, hold the belief that what they are telling people is belittling and shameful. Thoughts such as these become distressful because most people do not want to intentionally shame and belittle others, or to bring things to another's attention that will be perceived as being shameful and belittling. Yet we believe we have to do it.

These negative thoughts about the encounter blend with your internal physical arousal, and the result is experienced as feelings of embarrassment. Sometimes, the feeling is so intense that you will observe blushing of the face. These uncomfortable feelings influence how we act in the situation.

In this case, most people act out their embarrassment counterproductively. Some find the situation so embarrassing that their only way of managing it is to avoid giving the criticism. The trade-off here is that while you may avoid the embarrassment of the encounter, the odor remains.

Others attempt to manage the embarrassment of the situation by making believe it is not embarrassing. Typically, this has the paradoxical effect of making the situation even more embarrassing. This becomes evident as you sweat and stumble through the conversation.

How do you act out your embarrassment productively so that you can proceed to deliver the criticism? Act with emotional intelligence by self-disclosing that you are feeling embarrassed. Doing so allows you to bring out in the open the uncomfortable feelings you (and probably others) are experiencing about the encounter. In essence, the embarrassed feelings are no longer hidden, and their being out in the open allows you to confront and manage them productively.

In a broader sense, openly acknowledging the embarrassment provides you with the opportunity to learn how to deal with uncomfortable feelings. When you hide embarrassing feelings, or any distressful feeling, you may avoid them.

But, by avoiding your distressful feelings or encounters, you rob yourself of the opportunity to learn how to deal with them.

The simplest way to acknowledge that you are embarrassed is to say, "I find this to be embarrassing," or, "I feel embarrassed bringing this up, and you probably do, too." You will find that self-disclosing that you are embarrassed instantly reduces the tension of the situation. After you have handled the embarrassment of the situation by acknowledging it, you are now ready to deliver what is still sensitive information.

Step two is to begin the criticism in a way that protects the person's self-esteem. Remember that the emotion of embarrassment centers on shameful thoughts and feelings. You do not want the recipient to feel as if she is being belittled or shamed, as these thoughts will evoke hurt feelings and defensiveness.

An effective way to prevent the recipient from feeling belittled or shamed is to mention the criticized behavior as if the individual is unaware of it; if she is not aware, there is no reason to be embarrassed. Even if she is aware of her offensive odor, she now can save face by thanking you for something that she "was not aware of." "I'll take care of it immediately" is the usual response.

The third step is to make the criticism work-related. When you implement this step, you are overcoming the barrier that the criticism is personal and is therefore off-limits. By showing the recipient how her personal hygiene affects her results, you have made the criticism a performance issue, not a personal issue.

Putting the three steps together, criticizing a person for personal hygiene might sound like this:

> I'm embarrassed to have to tell you this, and I'm sure you may be embarrassed, too; nevertheless, I wanted to bring to your attention your personal hy-

giene. You are probably not aware that you have some body odor, and it's making it difficult for clients and coworkers to work closely with you. I thought you'd want me to bring it to your attention so you could take care of the matter.

If this formula still doesn't help you out, perhaps you do be better with the "perfume" approach. A group of secretaries couldn't stand the smell of one of their coworkers. All of them were reluctant to say anything for fear it would hurt their peer's feelings. One of them came up with a plan. They all chipped in for some expensive toiletries. The secretary who had the best relationship with the intended recipient drew the task of delivering the criticism, which was presented along these lines:

I am going to say something to you that embarrasses me and might embarrass you, but I am going to say it anyway. You might not be aware of it, but you have body odor. Please don't take it the wrong way. I wanted to tell you because it's becoming a problem. The other ladies notice it, too. Now, we like you and we wanted to show you that we are sincere, so we all got you a gift. Use it in good health.

A month later, the secretaries reported that their coworker was no longer fouling up their work. It could probably be said that the power of positive criticism helped the secretary achieve the sweet smell of success!

Criticism Among Equals

"You can't tell your coworker what to do or how to do his job. It's not your place," says a sixth-grade teacher. "And even if you do," she adds, "you're going to be told, 'Don't tell me what to do. You are not my boss.' "

This teacher's statement is something I've heard thousands of times and cogently points out the difficulty of criticizing a coworker: You do not have the organizational authority to tell your coworker what to do because the organizational structure places you at the same level, presumably in both job skills and job power, of decision-making authority.

This is in marked contrast to the superior-subordinate relationship in which the superior is granted organizational power to, if necessary, make the subordinate respond to the criticism (even if the subordinate disagrees) or experience negative consequences. Although it is not an uncommon occurrence for subordinates to argue with their supervisors when they believe a criticism is not justified, the result is usually compliance, at least overtly. True, the arguments may silently persist for several months or longer, but they are silent because the organizational rule is usually, "Don't argue with the boss; he can hurt you." In most cases, though, the arguments are short-lived.

Peers, on the other hand, have equal work power, making arguments not only permissible but expected in criticism encounters. The problem here is that, as is well known in psychological circles, when an argument between two people intensifies, each person becomes more and more ego-entrenched in her position, with self-esteem potentially threatened. This makes it difficult to resolve the disagreement because, to each person, giving in carries with it a loss of self-esteem. This is one of the reasons that power struggles are so common among peers and that a compromise is the standard solution—each needs to have her self-esteem protected. Thus, any criticism of coworkers that has the potential to cause an argument has little chance of being productive since coworkers will protect their self-esteem by defending their behavior, and their equal job power will justify their right to do so.

Moreover, it is not unlikely that when you criticize a coworker, your criticism will be met with anger simply because your peer perceives you as overstepping your boundaries or thinks that you are criticizing her out of a competitive need, a desire to show her up.

Nevertheless, it is a rare forty-eight hours if you do not have to criticize a coworker, especially in a team-oriented environment. To do so effectively, your strategy is to present your criticism in a way that not only makes it permissible—despite your equal work power—but also strips your coworker of his right to refuse your criticism on the grounds that you are not his boss.

In short, when you criticize a coworker, you must phrase your criticism in a way that simultaneously avoids arguments and builds cooperation. Here are some methods to help you deal with the difficulties of criticizing a coworker.

Create the Perception of a Common Goal. Delivering your criticism in terms of a common goal unites you and your coworker. It immediately helps you create for your coworker the perception that you have a common ground on which to relate and thus minimizes the possibility of an argument.

From your peer's point of view, a common goal means that you are both in the same boat, going in the same direction. There is little reason to resist. Having this perception, she feels less threatened; her need to compete to protect herself changes to a desire to help herself by cooperating with you.

The best way to implement this strategy is to practice Tip #5: Choose the Right Words. In this case, choose words and phrases that stress cooperation rather than competitiveness or blame. For example, "We can get our report done quickly if you firm up the statistical data while I edit the text" is bound to be more effective than "Unless you get moving faster on the statistics, I won't be able to finish the report on time" or "You are not doing the statistics section fast enough."

Emphasizing the common goal and using words like "we" and "our," which imply a sharing of credit for a job well done, reduce the harmful sense of competition and the chance of starting a nonproductive argument.

Equally important, using a cooperative vocabulary in a criticism situation has the effect of building cohesiveness and support among peers because nobody is blamed. Dissension is avoided, and the power of positive criticism can go to work.

Show How a Peer's Performance Affects Both of You. To be able to criticize a fellow worker productively, it is important to convince him that you are not intruding on his territory. Even though your criticism may be intended as helpful, the other person may think you are sticking your nose into something that is none of your business—that you are playing boss.

Your strategy now becomes showing your coworker that the behavior you are criticizing impacts both of you. Since you are both affected by the behavior in question and since you both stand to gain if the criticism is resolved—or both suffer negative consequences if it isn't—it becomes easier for your peer to hear the criticism as an offer to cooperate rather than as an order; in essence, you get your coworker to see it as "some of your business" rather than "none of your business."

You will find this strategy to be particularly useful when you are frequently working with the same person. For example, let's say your coworker is constantly late for sales presentations, leaving you to stumble through your presentations alone without all the pertinent facts. The conventional criticism would be "You're never on time, and it makes me look like a fool." A more effective phrasing would be something like: "It's important for both of us to be at the sales meetings on time. If one of us is late, it creates a bad impression and we both suffer."

By showing your peer how her actions affect you (and vice versa), you are showing how both of you can benefit if she acts on your criticism. This increases the chances that the criticism will be productive because you have forestalled the argument that you don't have a right to criticize. Also, highlighting the fact that your coworker (as well as you) will benefit indicates that your criticism is not (solely) coming out of self-interest. Thus, your coworker is more likely to respond positively.

Agree With or Support a Peer's Behavior but Refer to Significant Others—People More Important Than Yourself—Who Probably Won't. Underlying this strategy is the fact that a common and unproductive facet of communication between peers is the expression of blame. How often have you heard someone (if not yourself) say, "I would have had the report in on time, but Bob didn't get me the statistics on time." Perhaps your coworker didn't carry out his part of the assignment on schedule, but putting all of the blame on him merely sets up a destructive accusation-defense situation. Bob is hardly likely to accept the criticism, for if he does, he is implicitly accepting responsibility for the breakdown of the entire project. The only way he can protect his position (and his self-image) is to reject the criticism out of hand.

Although it is not very often that we can agree with or support the wrong idea, attitude, or behavior, of a coworker, when we can pretend to, it removes any implication of blame and provides a bridge with which to make your point in opposition to the behavior. This is exactly the purpose of the aforementioned strategy.

A research librarian noticed that her coworker did not return reference cards to their appropriate places until the end of the day or until she had a dozen or so that she could save time by returning them all at once. Although she did not want to play boss, she knew, and wanted to let her coworker know, that their boss wanted these cards put back immediately. She got her criticism across by agreeing with her coworker:

> I've noticed that you put the cards back at the end of the day. I agree that's easier and just as accurate. I used to do the same thing until I learned that the boss gets very annoyed if the cards aren't returned immediately. I think you'll save yourself a lot of trouble if you take my suggestion.

This comment made the criticizer an ally of the recipient. If her coworker was going to argue about the matter, she would have to do so with the boss. The beauty of this technique is that you usually end up being thanked for saving your coworker from the negative consequences you have tactfully pointed out.

A derivation of this procedure is to claim past agreement with your coworker's position. (Blame is never implied if you stress that you once felt the same way, until some clear or overwhelming evidence changed your opinion.) This means that you have put yourself on her side of the argument in the past and that you only gave up the positions she now holds after learning more. Actually, you are just dating your agreement to a prior time when you knew less about the subject or situation. Helpful phrases to use are "That's how it looked to me too, until . . ." or "I used to do it that way too, but . . ."

Ask for Permission to Criticize. Asking for permission to criticize your coworker is especially effective because it makes irrelevant the issue of whether you have the right to criticize—if you are granted permission, you gain the right. Ways of initiating this strategy are: "May I talk to you about something?" "May I make a suggestion?" "Do you have time to talk to me?" and "May I show you an easier way to do it?"

Many individuals have found this strategy extremely effective with defensive coworkers, since the act of giving permission commits the coworker to listening to what you are going to say. Occasionally, a coworker will respond along these lines: "No, I don't have time" or "I am not interested in what you think." When this occurs, the best response seems to be, "Is there a specific time when we can talk?" or "It's just a thought; you don't have to agree with me if you don't want to." If this doesn't move you closer to success, go back to the drawing board and be creative.

An underlying point that adds to the effectiveness of this technique is that if a person has given you permission to present an idea, he is more receptive than if the idea is presented without such permission. Furthermore, the mere fact of having asked permission not only protects his self-esteem but, in many cases, increases his self-esteem because it communicates that you respect him. Asking your coworker permission to criticize him takes advantage of these facts.

All of the aforementioned strategies have a common denominator: They avoid competitive patterns of relating, minimize the chance of arguments, and most importantly build cooperative relationships. Taken together, these points make it easier for you and your coworker to share the power of positive criticism.

In the Line of Fire

If there is one thing at work that you (or anyone else) doesn't need, it's a coworker or boss who makes an everyday practice of giving you unproductive critical comments about your work. This becomes a stressful situation because the constant barrage of negative criticism inevitably has negative effects on your performance, self-esteem, and feelings about your job. In fact, it is quite common for people who are subjected daily to a destructive critic to experience bouts of clinical depression. You could say that if you work with such a person, your mental health at work is dependent on effectively criticizing your destructive critic.

What doesn't work? Moving your desk, ignoring her remarks, or showing your displeasure. Rarely are these sufficient answers to this unpleasant problem.

A more effective strategy is to be like the akido expert who uses an opponent's power and applies reverse leverage to overcome him. The destructive critic is already criticizing you. Instead of trying to get him to stop criticizing you, encourage him to do so productively!

A window designer for a national retail company tells the story about her coworker who was always telling her negative things about how she displayed the store's merchandise in the window. "Sometimes the colors were wrong, other times the scene was too crowded, but most of the time it was, 'It looks lousy.' " The criticized window designer thought about her goal and formulated a way to best criticize her critical coworker. The next time she was faced with her coworker's critical comments, she asked her, "How can I do it better?"

This response aptly demonstrates how communicating criticism can be effectively reduced to one sentence. Look what happens. If the negative criticizer tells you what you've asked, you are the winner. On the other hand, if the response is along the lines of "I don't know," your best bet is to explain, "I'm doing the best I can. I would appreciate it if you would keep your criticisms to yourself until you can tell me how to do it better because, after all, I do welcome your productive criticism." In effect, you are not telling your coworker not to criticize you; rather, you are asking her to change how she criticizes you.

If her critical comments continue, be more direct. You can point out that while productive criticism is appropriate, her being constantly and unproductively critical is not helping you do your job, nor is it making you feel good, and you are not quite sure why she is engaging in such destructive behavior. Let her know that if the behavior continues, you will ask for a meeting with the boss and will request that she also be present.

Of course, it is wise to suggest that an alternative is the two of you sitting down together and making a cooperative effort to better the situation. The second choice is usually picked. The fact that you even offer this as an option also serves to show your coworker that you want to have a good working relationship with her. However, while going to your boss may make you uncomfortable, it may be what it takes in some cases to make your life easier.

A derivation of this strategy is particularly helpful with a boss who is almost always (and exclusively) pointing out what you do wrong. Since a governing rule for the boss-subordinate relationship is that you don't tell the boss what to do, your response to unproductive criticism would be to structure the criticism process.

Ask your boss to set aside a time in which he can criticize you productively. Instruct him as to which areas of your work you wish to have criticized. Emphasize that knowing what he likes is just as important to you as knowing what he thinks needs to be improved. Assuming that all goes well (or at least better) in this productive session, at the end of the meeting express your sense of the benefits of the session and your desire to have such sessions on a continuing basis, regardless of how infrequently—and remember to implement his valid criticisms. In essence, you are teaching your boss how to get the power of positive criticism. Everybody wins!

Criticism in Groups

At a nursing staff meeting, a head nurse has to criticize one of her subordinates for the way she is treating a patient. An advertising executive reviews a layout with a client, an artist, and two copywriters; he criticizes the artist. An engineer presents a software system to his colleagues. They find several glitches and criticize his oversights.

All of these situations represent one of the most difficult criticism encounters—giving criticism in a public forum, whether it is a staff or team meeting. At the very least, the recipient is usually embarrassed. And the giver runs the risk of injecting tension into the meeting, which all too often inhibits others from contributing their thoughts. Why take a chance if you might be criticized? (It is likely your staff has a negative definition of criticism.) Risk-taking behavior and innovation are stifled.

Yet, criticizing an individual (and being criticized) in a group or public setting is a reality of work. What seems to make it a particularly stressful experience is that it goes against conventional wisdom that says criticism should be given privately. While this opinion is usually valid, the above situations and hundreds of others frequently demand that criticism be given in front of others. If this be your task, I know of two strategies that can serve you well.

The first is to *depersonalize* the criticism by specifically directing comments to the work per se, not to the person who performed it. For example, the advertising executive would depersonalize his criticism by proclaiming, "Let's look at the layout; I think the graphics need to be more colorful" rather than specifically addressing the artist by saying, "The layout is good; I think you need to make your graphics more color-ful." The first phrasing focuses on the layout itself, while the second singles out the artist as the person who didn't do his part.

When using this strategy, pay attention to behavioral lo-gistics. Imagine, for instance, that you are the advertising ex-ecutive. You would put the layout on the table and have your staff sit around it. You would then "interact" with the graph-ics by pointing to them and making your criticisms at the same time. By acting in this manner, you focus attention on the work rather than on the individual who created it. The overall effect is to make the responsible individual more ob-jective because you have detached him from the criticism in-teraction. You have made your recipient an observer (just like everyone else in the group) rather than a direct participant.

This strategy is effectively used by a major company in the communications technology business. In one of the com-pany's research labs for developing software programs, the developers must have their work inspected by their col-leagues. As you can imagine, the review process is loaded with criticisms. Their procedure adopts this strategy by hav-ing the inspecting computer experts sit around a table, each with a copy of the software program. A moderator reads the document, and each inspector offers criticism in turn. The moderator makes sure that the inspectors address their criti-cisms to the document, not its designer. The actual developer is also present but sits away from the table. Her task is solely to listen and make notes. The behavioral logistics of her sit-ting away from the table helps everyone remember to focus on the software and, at the same time, helps the designer listen more objectively because although she is present, she is removed from the direct process of being criticized.

Let me give you a second and more subtle way of offer-ing criticism to an individual in a group setting; turn the indi-vidual criticism into a group criticism by making the statement general. Let's suppose that, at a staff meeting, a head nurse is reviewing the treatment of the patients on the ward. When the name of a particular patient comes up, she wants to criticize the nurse assigned to him for not spending enough time with him. In fact, the nurse in question spends too little time with all her patients.

Instead of criticizing the nurse directly in front of her coworkers, which will probably elicit a defensive reaction such as, "Well, he tells me not to bother him" or "I have too many patients," the head nurse can handle the situation by making this general statement: "It's really important that we all spend adequate time with our patients. It is something we value here and is one reason people come to this hospital." A statement such as this serves several purposes. One is that it communicates to the nurse in question that it is indeed important to spend time with patients without letting her coworkers know that she is falling short of expected standards. Another is that it emphasizes the desirability of the same behavior to the other nurses; this is a bonus. If others in the room are spending adequate time with patients, it reinforces their behavior. If they are not, then they too profit from the criticism.

The pitfall of this strategy is that the recipient may not perceive that she is performing the criticized behavior and thus would not apply the statement to her own behavior. Nevertheless, contrast this technique with the option of creating a roomful of red, embarrassed faces, and defensive responses, and you'll see that the benefits outweigh the risk.

A related criticism situation is one in which business demands that you criticize a group of workers. Examples are criticizing a small team for how they handled a project and criticizing an entire division for poor quality control. In these situations, use the same principles as those for giving general criticism. Be specific, be encouraging, and express a vote of confidence in the group's ability to get the job done.

One particular strategy to use when criticizing a group is to apply Tip #6, and use a metaphor. Not only does the metaphor provide the means for communicating the criticism, but a group metaphor also builds cohesiveness, a quality that is apt to facilitate the functioning—and thus improve the results—of the group.

A famed basketball coach found success when he criticized his team for not getting along. They were constantly bickering and blaming each other for team losses. He criticized them like this:

> You know, a basketball team is just like a hand. [He holds up his hand as he gives the criticism.] Look . . . every hand has five fingers. Each finger can pretty well do as it wants. But the hand only has use when the fingers work together. When the fingers work together, they have strength. But if the big finger yells at the pinky, and if the index finger ignores the thumb, then the hand is nothing. Even if the fingers are strong, smaller hands will have a stronger grip . . . because the fingers must work together to become a hand.

Remember that criticizing a group through metaphor is not for everybody. It usually takes very good communicative skills and a motivational style of delivery, since the members of the group have to believe in the metaphor if they are to relate it to their particular situation.

Another tactic to try when criticizing a group is to present the criticism in a manner that forces the group members to come up with the answer to the problem and resolve the criticism themselves. Instead of "You guys are really screwing things up," "The quality of the department's product stinks," "You better all shape up, or you might all be out of a job," try: "Listen. The quality of the department's product is way down. What do you all think can be done to improve it?"

This is an application of Tip #11, Use Questions Socratically. It is effective with group members not only because they usually come up with an answer that makes sense but also because the group problem solving makes them a more cohesive unit. Each individual becomes integrated into the problem-solving process. The team becomes revitalized and begins to apply peer pressure on each other to implement the solution and resolve the criticism.

Now, let's turn the tables. What if you are the one being criticized in a group setting? What is your best response? Certainly, you know it is not to get defensive, even if you are being wronged. Practice Tip #20: Stay Cool, Calm, and Collected. You can think on your feet and decide your best course of action.

The acceptable range includes: sitting quietly and taking notes on what you are being told; assertively asking your critic to be more specific and asking his thoughts as to how to make the situation better; or quickly acknowledging the validity of the criticism and moving on.

If you think your critic is getting carried away, point out that others in the group might not be interested in this discussion and that you two can continue to discuss it afterwards. If he still persists, simply thank your critic in front of others for trying to give you the power of positive criticism.

"I Lost It in the Sun"

It can be pretty frustrating to have to deal with an excuse maker. Every time you criticize her, that's what you hear—an excuse to explain the results achieved.

Sometimes, it's as plain as "It's not my fault." Other times, it's a little more pointed: "Gee, Jack didn't get me the data on time . . . that's why the report is late." Or it's more elaborate: "Well, I spoke to the sales agent about three weeks ago, and he was supposed to call me back. When I didn't hear from him . . ." In either case, the result is the same: Your recipient in effect denies your criticism because the reason that he gives is intended to justify his actions. Thus, "I know I was supposed to have the report finished on Thursday, but Mr. Smith gave me another assignment" really means "The report wasn't supposed to be finished on Thursday because Mr. Smith gave me something else to do." Put another way, your recipient is simply pointing out that she is not responsible for her results, and thus your evaluation of the situation is unjust.

Why a person makes an excuse differs on an individual basis, but there are two main theories that are thought to generate the majority of excuses you hear. The first is that the excuse maker is coming from a position of being insecure. To him, if he admits he is responsible, he thinks he is a failure. Making excuses becomes his way of protecting his self-esteem.

The second theory for excuse making is simply that the excuse has become an effective way for the individual to avoid responsibility for her actions. The fact that the excuses have helped the individual avoid responsibility for her actions is what makes it a repetitive response to criticism.

Regardless of what theory is in action, the strategy is the same: Minimize the chance that the individual will make excuses for his results so that he can realistically look at his work and begin to improve. There are several ways you can handle the task, each geared to a theory of excuse making.

The first approach stems from treating the excuse behavior as a defensive behavioral pattern of responding that has been used effectively over a period of time. When this is the case, the first sign of criticism triggers an excuse; your recipient will quickly interrupt you with what has become her automatic response: "Yes, but . . ." The plan here is to break the defensive pattern.

Do this by voicing your criticisms, and before your recipient has a chance to respond, ask her to think about it for a few days. The theory is that slowing down her response will allow her to appraise the criticism more accurately and recognize her responsibility in the situation at hand.

Appropriate phrasing of this approach would be: "Listen, I am going to tell you something, but I don't want you to respond now. I want you think it over for a few days; and then we will discuss it at the end of the week." In this phrasing, you short-circuit the excuse maker by telling her not to respond.

Underlying this technique is whether or not you are criticizing a boss or subordinate. If you are the boss, you can effectively use this technique. You can subtly order your subordinates to delay his response so that he can thoughtfully reflect on what you are saying. Because you are the boss, you will get little resistance. If you do, quickly hold up your hands and reiterate that you are not going to discuss the matter until he has thought about it for a few days. He will get the message. You may have to use this approach several times, but after a while, you will start to see the excuse maker making less and less excuses. This occurs because he is learning to befriend criticism. Getting him to delay his excuse-making response not only increases his awareness and makes him more effective on the job but also allows him to develop a new and more productive way of responding to criticisms from other resources, too.

On the other hand, if you are the subordinate, you might be a little uncomfortable telling your boss or peer that you want her to think about something for several days before she responds to you. The same might be true for criticizing your client. Since they either have authority over you or are paying you for your services, these recipients typically believe they have the right to immediately respond to what you say; their relationship to you gives them this right. Thus, use this approach carefully with your boss or client. Remember, though, the better your working relationship is, the more likely it is that your toughest recipients will delay their response, and thus increase the likelihood that they will respond nondefensively.

A second approach to the excuse maker is based on the theory that excuse making comes out of insecurity. This dictates the strategy that your best bet is simply to acknowledge to your recipient that it is permissible to make mistakes and that while you expect her to function at her optimal level, you do not expect her to be perfect.

With appropriate conviction on your part, the message makes the subordinate feel that she does not have to prove that she is not at fault every time she is criticized. It is also good policy to point out that mistakes provide a good opportunity to learn how to do something better. When you use this approach, you are giving permission to fail, which paradoxically is an important component of building the recipient's confidence to handle new situations and to attempt new and challenging tasks.

A third, and what I consider to be the most direct, way of dealing with the excuse maker is to forget about why the excuses occur and simply criticize the individual directly for constantly making excuses for his results. This can be combined with the delay tactic mentioned above:

> Listen, I want to tell you something and I don't want you to respond now . . . I want you to think it over. Most of the time when I criticize you, you have reasons for why something didn't happen as planned. A lot of times, those reasons make sense. But rarely—I can't think of one time, maybe you can—do I recall your saying that it was your responsibility or that you made a mistake. I find this makes it hard for me to help you develop because part of developing is acknowledging that you make mistakes. I also think that it prevents you from fairly evaluating your own strengths. Don't respond now. Think about it, and we will discuss it later on in the week.

Several points are at play here. First, the boss pointed out that some of the subordinate's excuses were valid; failure to do this would probably cause your recipient to cite examples of legitimate excuses and thus discredit the overall criticism.

At the same time, she stated that although there have been legitimate excuses, she couldn't think of any times when the subordinate took responsibility, and she invited the subordinate to cite one. This is a neat way to imply "always" without actually saying "always," a word that usually triggers defensiveness.

The third point to note is that the superior did not lean too hard on the subordinate; rather, she implied that she sees the subordinate as someone who has the ability to develop, but only if he takes responsibility for his results. This puts the subordinate in a bind: The only way he can improve is to acknowledge that he is responsible for results.

Finally, anytime an excuse maker owns up to his results, remember not to reprimand him for making a mistake. This is equivalent to punishing a five-year-old child for telling you the truth (you can bet he will choose to lie next time). Instead, reinforce his change by telling him how much you appreciate his taking responsibility for the results and quickly move on to discussing how to improve the situation. When you respond like this, you let your recipient know that once he accepts responsibility for his results, he is using the power of positive criticism to make things better.

When the Customer Isn't Right

Have you ever had to criticize your best customer or client? Most people hesitate to perform that task because they fear their criticism will offend their client and cause the client to go elsewhere. In other words, they fear losing the client's business.

"The customer is always right" may be your company credo, but we all know this is far from the truth. And we all know that there are plenty of times when to do your job right, you have to criticize the customer.

Your best strategy is to phrase the criticism so it reflects your desire to provide what every customer and client wants—better service. When this approach is taken, it becomes nonoffensive and immediately lets the customer know that changing her behavior is in her best interest because it will get her better service, which is what you want to provide.

I witnessed a perfect implementation of this approach at a major metropolitan airport. A ticket agent dealt with an overbearing customer by telling him, "Sir, if you just calm down and answer my questions, I will be able to take care of you right away. Otherwise, you might miss your plane!" The customer regained his composure, provided only the necessary information, got his ticket, and thanked the agent. Imagine the consequences if the ticket agent had responded to the same customer with anger, defensiveness, and poor service.

This "Let me give you better service" strategy is also applicable to more long-term relationships, such as when the client continually acts in a way that negatively affects your work. A junior partner in a Big Six accounting firm once had a client who was consistently late in reporting his tax information. This caused the accountant to file extensions, which his superiors did not want him to do. Although the client was influential, the accountant finally criticized him by saying, "If you can get your tax information to me earlier this year, I can devote more time to your returns and save you more money. Also, I won't have to keep filing extensions, so there will be less chance of an audit." The client responded by making sure that this information was given to the accountant on a timely, periodic basis, and the accountant's superior noted that the accountant was destined for partnership.

This is a good time to reiterate two points: The same criticism can be phrased in many different ways, and if the criticism is not effective, change the incentive.

Another accountant in the same firm told me of a similar client who not only was late in providing his tax information but was also very disorganized. After having no luck in motivating the client with the promises of less taxes and avoiding an audit (strategies used by his colleague), he tried a different approach.

Knowing the client for several years, he had come to learn that the client's ten-year-old daughter was his pride and joy. As a result, he criticized his client by saying, "Boy, you are going to be very unhappy if your daughter is as disorganized as you." The accountant reported that his client immediately became better organized and more punctual filing his information.

Sometimes, it is absolutely necessary to criticize a customer, even if the criticism cannot be disguised as a route to better customer service and you run the risk of offending the customer or losing her.

In a seminar, a flight attendant volunteered her story that a passenger was flirting with her in a most obnoxious way to the point where other passengers noticed and seemed to be feeling uncomfortable. She took action by saying, loud enough for others to hear, "Sir, will you please mind your manners." She told us, "He was a perfect gentleman for the rest of the trip." In this case, the flight attendant had strong grounds for criticizing; she not only stopped a disruptive behavior but also let the other passengers know that she was in charge, a perception that makes passengers more comfortable.

There are other times when you criticize the customer because you find his behavior unacceptable and simply do not want his business if the behavior continues. A manager of a computer store recounts such an experience:

A customer called up complaining about his computer printer. My service department tried to help him over the phone, but he kept saying, yelling actually, that he couldn't understand them—both service engineers are Korean. He became very abusive, and the call was passed on to me. I tried to help him over the phone and instruct him on what to do, but to no avail. He asked about a service call; because he lived only a few minutes away from the store, I made the visit myself. I wanted to speak to him.

When I got there, I fixed the printer—all it needed was a new ribbon cartridge. Apparently, when my service department told him to pick up the "cover" of the printer, he thought they were saying "coover" and had no idea what they were talking about. Anyway, when he asked how much the service call was, I told him to forget it and that I wanted to talk to him. I said, "Listen, my service department, as is the case with all my employees, does excellent work. The two gentlemen you spoke to are Korean, and they both do excellent work and provide excellent service. They are both learning English as best and as fast as they can. In fact, for most people, their English is not a problem. I want you to know that my staff is very important to me, and if you can't treat them with respect, then I would prefer that you go to another store." He became very apologetic and agreed that his behavior had been inappropriate. He even said he would call the service people and apologize. I told him that wasn't necessary, that I just wanted to let him know that my staff is very important to me and I expect customers to treat them with respect. Two days later, he walked into the store and apologized to the two Korean gentlemen. To top it off, he has remained our customer.

What is important here is that the manager, personal values aside, decided it was appropriate to criticize a customer and run the risk of losing him. He evaluated the situation to be very important and decided that if the customer was going to continue behaving abusively toward his staff, it would be better to lose the customer than to force his staff to tolerate such behavior.

By criticizing the customer (and he told his staff he was going to do that before he made his service call), he demonstrated to his staff that while the customer is important, he is not so important that the boss would let him abuse his staff. He used criticizing the customer as a means of building employee loyalty and protected his staff's self-esteem in the process. And let's not forget that he changed the customer's behavior, too. No doubt, this manager computed the power of positive criticism.

"That's a Terrible Idea";
"It Won't Work";
"Nobody Cares"

One of the most miserable experiences that people report having at work is working with a person who is constantly displaying a negative attitude, usually in the form of constant complaining or comments that discourage and demotivate his coworkers. A manager at a pharmaceutical company describes the experience of working with such an individual:

> At first, his negativity isn't so bad because you hear it as some valid complaints. But after a while, it gets to you. It becomes more than just complaining. It is a constant voicing of negative comments about everything—projects, the company, other departments, even the customers. And many of the comments have nothing to do with work per se. We could be talking about a company picnic and the guy will say, "It's probably going to rain." Or, we could be getting a division softball team together and he'll say, "Nobody's going to want to play." After a while, you find that you want to avoid this guy; you don't want to work with him. And when you do, you end up feeling discouraged, demotivated, and powerless. Anytime you are with him, you feel down. A team can be excited about a project and then Mr. Negativity points out, "It will never work; it's too

hard to do." No matter what others say, he is negative.

I've noted that these types of responses kill my team's motivation. Even more troublesome, the team begins to exhibit a negative attitude. They begin to complain; they become cynical and less motivated. The end result is that the whole team becomes less productive. It's like a disease, an epidemic—everybody catches negativity symptoms. It's amazing. This one guy created a sea of negativity. And you know, if I'm around the guy too long, I begin to feel dejected, too.

The manager is right. His staff did catch the negativity of their coworker, and it is the catching of this negativity that makes it so difficult to work with a person who has a negative attitude: It brings us down. We become negative too, and our work suffers accordingly. Indeed, it is his negative impact on our behavior and those around us that prompts our need to criticize.

Considering there are so many people who spend their working hours telling others, "It's not going to work," "Nobody really cares," "I've tried that before," "You will never be able to pull it off," and making other comments that communicate a negative attitude, it is not surprising that how to deal with such a person is a standard on so many people's "most difficult criticism list."

How do you criticize a person who is always negative and always complaining? You must first immunize yourself against catching the negative affect that your recipient engenders. Take the manager's words literally: You do catch the negativity from your coworker through a process called emotional contagion.

Researchers in the study of emotions have demonstrated that many emotions—anger, fear, anxiety, depression, enthusiasm—are contagious. Like a social virus, they literally spread from one individual to another. How this happens requires an elaborate understanding of the process, but suffice it to say that emotions are transferred through sound, facial expressions, and body gestures. As a matter of fact, when we are with others, we often mimic their behavior, voice pattern, and facial expressions; this mimicry is usually beyond our conscious awareness. The last time a stranger smiled at you and your smiling back illustrates the point. Raising your voice in response to someone's yelling at you is another example we all have experienced. Or, think of a staff meeting that began with a complaint or two and then ballooned into a gripe session. Emotional contagion was at work.

When you frequently work with a negative person, you begin to catch her negativity. You begin to think like her ("It won't work") and feel as she does (low level of energy); your performance, like hers, declines. In essence, emotional contagion has made you a negative person, too. Unless, of course, you have immunized yourself against catching her symptoms.

To immunize yourself from the negativity of others, first *anticipate* your meetings with the person in question, and clarify your own thoughts and feelings about your work. Doing so allows you to bring into your awareness that the negativity is the other individual's, not yours.

For example, while your coworker might be negative about the team project, you recognize that you are quite positive. By being tuned in to how you are thinking and feeling about the team project, you prevent yourself from being overly influenced by the negative thoughts and feelings that are headed your way. By anticipating the meeting, you can then think of a strategy of how best to deal with the encounter, something you are unable to do if you catch his negative emotions. When you do not anticipate that you are going to be bombarded with negative affect, you are caught off guard; before long, you are feeling negative, too.

Using *instructional self-statements* also helps: "Just because he's negative doesn't mean that I have to feel discouraged"; "No matter how negative she is, I will be positive." These self-statements are powerful immunization shots because they increase your cognitive awareness of what the other individual is experiencing and guide you in how best to respond. In effect, your awareness of your thoughts minimizes your chances of subconsciously mimicking the behaviors—and thoughts—that transmit contagious emotions. (You would be wise to write down several instructional self-statements that you could say to yourself when you are encountering a negative person. Keep them in a place that makes them easy to use.)

Once you have immunized yourself against catching your coworker's negativity, you are ready to perform the second step; delivering the criticism. This can be tricky because in contrast to the person who is giving you negative criticism, the negative person is not directly speaking to you. His negativity is generalized toward everything. Thus, if you criticize him too directly, he will use your criticism to confirm that "Everyone around here is negative, especially you."

The situation is not insurmountable if you have the right criticism goal. In this case, it is to bring into the individual's awareness that he projects negativity and that this negativity is not serving him well. This awareness often gets the individual to contain some of his negative comments.

Also, since the individual is not criticizing you directly, your best move is to weave the criticism into a daily encounter rather than formalizing it in your office at 10:30. Weaving it into a daily encounter allows you to present the criticism as a more benign observation, which is necessary so the negative person doesn't interpret your criticism as being more bad vibes.

Here is how you might say it as you are leaving a staff meeting in which your team was once again swept away with negativity that was initiated by your coworker, Jack:

> Hey Jack, just my observation, but I think the way you are coming across in staff meetings might not be in your best interest. You may not be aware of the fact that many of your coworkers interpret your responses as a negative attitude. I'm sure you can think of some more effective ways to voice your thoughts so that the important concerns you have can be addressed.

Highlighting this criticism is the message that the negativity is harmful to Jack's performance, rather than making him responsible for the feelings and actions of others (i.e., "Your negative attitude is affecting others"). It also protects his self-esteem by raising the possibility that he may not even be aware that he is projecting negativity. Finally, it is improvement-oriented by suggesting he can be more effective.

It would be naive to think that every person with a negative attitude would productively respond to the above or some similarly said criticism. If they don't, you might find success with the technique of criticism through self-confrontation. Using this technique requires you to phrase the criticism in a way that causes the individual to confront herself about how and why she is operating in the way she does. Some examples:

> "I'm not sure why you want to say negative comments at a staff meeting when you know it makes the meeting counterproductive."
>
> "It might be a good idea for you to think about why you do things that always alienate others and get yourself in trouble."
>
> "I'm surprised you want to work here, considering you think everything is so bad."

These criticisms are high impact: They immediately call for the negative person to increase awareness about what she is doing and why. Sometimes, but rarely, the individual will conclude that her best move is to get out, "You know, you're right. I should leave this situation and I will."

However, the majority of times, the criticism makes your recipient uncomfortable because it forces her to confront the fact that she is choosing to stay in a bad situation or choosing to act counterproductively. This is especially disconcerting for the bright individual. Not wanting to leave his job nor wanting to make things worse, the recipient searches for ways to make the situation he is in more tolerable. The common response is that he reappraises the situation and realizes it is not that bad. He stops being so negative.

While stopping the person's negativity is surely a positive outcome, your third step in the process is to realize that you are still short of the ultimate goal: to help the person be transformed into a positive person.

To apply this step, be aware that people who project negativity typically have low self-esteem. They feel badly about themselves, and their negativity is simply a reflection of those feelings. Your task here is to build up their self-esteem; in so doing, you will note that they will not only begin to delete their negative comments but also begin to generate positive ones.

Building up a persons' self-esteem does not require you to be a psychotherapist. Simply tune into the daily opportunities in which you can show the individual that he counts. Show him his ideas are important to you by requesting his input in the early stages of a project. Doing so also allows you to preempt his negativity. Ask him to identify what is wrong and to problem-solve how he can overcome the barriers (this makes use of his negativity). Praise him when he makes positive comments. At staff meetings, make sure he feels included. Ask for his thoughts; when possible, encourage him to take responsibility for important team tasks.

Obviously, acting in the above manner assumes that you truly want to help the individual change his attitude. While the effort may seem taxing to you, remember the bottom line is that your efforts will be rewarded. As your coworker transforms into an individual with a positive attitude, your work encounters with him will be more productive. You will also feel more energized, and so will all the other individuals who have to work with him. Your efforts will benefit all. You will know you have reached your ultimate goals when you observe Mr. Negativity giving the power of positive criticism to others!

When You're the Fall Guy

For most of us, being criticized by our boss for something that our subordinates or peers did quickly evokes anger. We see the criticism as being unjust—we believe we are being held responsible for the actions of others. Adding to the anger is our appraisal that our boss must know nothing of the situation if she is misdirecting her criticism to us instead of directing it to the individuals who deserve it.

While your reaction may be justified, it would be a huge error to tell your boss her evaluation is off because it is your subordinates' fault. Shifting blame and making excuses won't help; they are repugnant to most bosses. More important, the organizational structure makes your subordinates' performance ultimately your responsibility and yours alone. Blaming subordinates will only suggest to your boss that you are not able to manage them effectively.

It is much wiser for you to be the perfect fall guy: Agree with your superior and accept the responsibility. Besides, what needs to be discussed is not between you and your boss; the necessary discussion is the one between you and your subordinates.

Simply use the boss's criticism as information to increase your awareness about why the job wasn't done to expected standards. With this in mind, you can explore with your subordinates the boss's criticism of the work/incident and then use productive criticism to motivate them so that the incident is not likely to occur again.

When your coworkers are involved, two different situations are possible. One is when your peers deserve to be criticized along with you. The other is when your peers deserve to be criticized instead of you.

In the first case, tell your boss that you agree with the criticism and that you will respond appropriately. Then recommend that she share the criticism with your peers, since they would benefit, too. This is a good way to get your coworkers to hear the criticism without being an office snitch. On the side, you can approach these coworkers, share the criticism you received, and work out a plan so you can all avoid the criticism in the future. This usually works.

A district manager of a large food chain passed on the criticism he received from his regional manager to his peers this way:

> Listen. George is very disappointed that we as a district have not been getting our produce into our stores fast enough. He says we are all responsible. He recommended that we look into how we route the produce and how fast our suppliers get the stuff to us. To me, that is a good idea. I am already getting my routes checked out. You might want to do the same.

Note that the district manager who passed on the criticism simply communicated the information, using cooperative words—we, our, us. Most important, he did not attempt to tell the coworkers what to do (it was not his criticism) but simply told them how he personally was going to respond. If you find sharing the criticism doesn't work, improve your skill at peer criticism; at the same time, let your boss know that you personally are responding to the criticism.

The second situation—when your peers deserve to be criticized instead of you—is trickier. It may be best (you will have to size up the situation yourself) to accept criticism anyway and promise to respond to it. Any other response may be seen as defensiveness or an attempt to put blame on your coworkers. Although you are taking the heat for something you didn't do, you are also showing your boss that you can accept responsibility. After all, your boss might be giving out the same criticism to other innocent coworkers, too. And besides, she may feel you are culpable because you are part of the team. However, if this response is not acceptable to you, then react by making the boss be very specific: "Well, what are you basing this on?" "I am not quite sure why I am responsible for this," or "Are you saying that this was my responsibility?" Statements like these will help your boss clarify exactly what your role is in the situation and perhaps see that you are being unfairly evaluated.

Whichever tack you take, ask your boss to pass the criticism on to the others. This way, you can make sure that your peers get to take advantage of the power of positive criticism too.

Friendship Harassment

Making friends at work can be a mixed blessing. It's an attractive arrangement to be working with someone whom you like and are able to socialize with after-hours. But for many people, the relationship sours as soon as criticism needs to be given at work. A seminar participant recalled his scenario along these lines:

> "Hey John, when you go over that report, make sure you redo the graphs. They really need to be fixed up. What were you doing, watching TV or something when you were doing them?"
>
> "No! I think they're fine. Anyway, what the hell are you doing, giving me more work to do. I thought your last report stunk and I kept my mouth shut!"
>
> "That's not true. My report was good."
>
> "Fine, if you think so. I thought it could have been much better. The point is, I don't tell you what to do. I expect the same, friend!"

Most people say that criticizing a coworker whom they've become friendly with is especially stressful because the criticism will be disruptive to the friendship, which is usually of value to both parties. Furthermore, now that you're friends with your coworker, she expects you to look the other way or let her do as she pleases, even if you are the boss. Unfortunately, keeping your criticism to yourself may preserve your friendship, but at the same time, it impedes your effectiveness at work.

You could suggest that criticizing a friend at work can

be avoided simply by not making friends at work. However, considering that most people spend at least a third of their day in their working environment, this suggestion would be extreme. Not only is it natural to make friends at work, but many people go to work specifically hoping that they will make friends with their fellow employees.

You could also avoid criticizing friends at work by choosing your friends at work carefully, paying particular attention to where they are in the organizational hierarchy and what they can do for you. The more influential they are, the less you criticize. But it has been my experience that if you act on this recommendation, you keep your criticisms to yourself for fear of being offensive and losing your contacts. Furthermore, you are going against what is known to be true—criticism needs to be voiced for individuals and organizations to do their best. More important, these criteria are hardly the basis for a friendship. People who base their friendships on job status and connections are usually perceived as manipulative and untrustworthy, two qualities that create enemies rather than friends.

Therefore, since it is the inevitable that you will make friends at work, and since you will no doubt have to criticize them, the following two pointers for criticizing friends at work are proposed:

1. Since thoughts affect behavior, clarify your attitude about making friends at work. If you believe that friends and work don't mix, your best bet is to make friends elsewhere, since you are sure to create problems for yourself. If you think you can handle the dilemmas that friends at work may bring and that friendship is worth the problems it may cause, then feel free to make as many friends as you can, regardless of their job status.
2. When you have to criticize a friend, use the friendship to facilitate the criticism rather than letting it be an

obstacle to the criticism. Do this by beginning with a statement along these lines: "One of the nice things about being friends is that you are able to communicate openly and honestly, even when it comes to criticism." You may even add that you wouldn't be a very good friend if you didn't help her do her work more effectively. While this sounds a bit sugar-coated, remember that it is the phrasing of the point that makes it effective; be sure to tailor your phrasing of these thoughts to each particular situation.

A broker reported that he had criticized a close friend he worked with about the way he dressed by starting out with, "Look, we're friends, right? You want me to give you the truth or a bunch of B.S.?" For insurance, throw in that, as a friend, you certainly expect to have the same attitude when it comes to criticizing you.

This approach is extremely effective for two reasons. First, it is intellectually appealing. It is very hard for the recipient to make a case against you for telling her something that can help her, even if the information might be initially distressing. Second, it forces the recipient to acknowledge that you are criticizing her because you care about her. This helps minimize defensiveness and allows your friend to evaluate your criticism more accurately. If your friend plays wise guy and says, "Give me the B.S.," simply effuse on what a good job she is doing. She'll get the point.

Making friends at work can not only make your job more enjoyable but can also enhance your success, especially when you and your friends decide to give each other the power of positive criticism.

When Criticism Is Ethical

One of the most trying experiences that people have at work is observing something that goes against their personal ethics. Some examples:

- ◊ A bank teller seeing a loan officer stretching the rules so the customer, who is the loan officer's friend, can get a loan
- ◊ A sales rep witnessing a coworker padding his business expenses from his recent trip
- ◊ An electrician knowing that her boss is recommending a particular type of wire to a customer because it is more expensive than another type that is equally good for the project
- ◊ An employee hearing the president of the company touting the company's stock even though business is bad
- ◊ A nurse seeing a doctor suggesting a particular operation for financial reasons instead of medical reasons

These situations are often anger-provoking because the other person's actions clash with your own sense of right and wrong—you see the person intentionally doing something that you know is blatantly wrong. Indeed, one of the functions of anger is to mobilize your resources so that you can correct an unjust situation, in this case, the unethical behavior.

However, the situation becomes more complicated when you consider that these behaviors reflect ethical judgments. What one person defines as unethical may be perfectly acceptable to his colleague. These judgments are traditionally thought of as a personal matter and thus not appropriate to criticize. In effect, to voice your criticism is trying to instill your ethics in someone else. Good luck.

When you finally do criticize (sometimes it takes awhile for the anger to get you to act), the usual response is either "Look, mind your own business" or "You do what you think is right, and I will do the same."

The exception, of course, is if you are the boss criticizing a subordinate. In that case, you can use your authority, if need be, to prevent the criticized (unethical) behavior from recurring. If you are not the boss, what then? And what do you do if it's your immediate boss or someone higher up who, in your eyes, is acting unethically? There are three choices to ponder.

The first is to do nothing. Get angry, but manage it by talking to your friends, maybe even a few coworkers; in the end, say nothing. You simply accept the situation and perhaps think, "Well, that's the way she is. It is not the way I am." The key point is to acknowledge that you are free to set your own ethical standards as others will do for themselves. Equally important, while you may not voice your criticism, you can still learn from it; in this case, you may get some valuable information as to how this person may act in future business situations.

The second choice is to quit your job. If you find the situation unbearable, you can always leave. Being able to implement this choice obviously depends on whether you need the job, whether you can find a new job, and whether any other problems would result.

The third choice is to voice your criticism to the person involved. The drawback here is not that you will be told that you are out of line but that, in some extreme cases, you may get fired. Indeed, I have heard many stories over the years in which this was the case, but most of the time, those fired state: "I didn't care whether or not I got fired. I just knew I couldn't live with any self-respect if I didn't say anything." This illustrates an important point about criticizing unethical behavior: Do what you must, but be prepared to accept the consequences of your decision. It may be that the power of positive criticism puts you out of your job.

I Heard It Through the Grapevine

A sales rep for a computer company was told by another sales rep that she had heard the first sales rep's work wasn't up to par. When the first rep asked who the source of the criticism was, her coworker stated, "I don't remember. I heard it a few days ago."

A lab technician at a hospital had a similar experience. His coworker had "promised not to reveal the source." Both the criticized sales rep and lab technician reported that the experience made them very "nervous that people were saying things behind my back . . . angry because I wasn't told whom to speak to."

Situations like these—hearing a criticism about yourself through a third party—are extremely frequent in the working world because it is less confrontational and anxiety-arousing to criticize a person behind her back (indirectly) than criticizing the person directly. In fact, many of the criticisms that we say behind a person's back are those that we would never communicate to the person directly. We are more comfortable saying it to others, as when we criticize our boss when speaking to our assistant or criticizing a client when speaking to a coworker.

Sometimes, we do this just to vent our thoughts and feelings; other times, we intentionally do it because we are hoping that the information will get back to the intended recipient. Regardless of our motive, though, the initiator of secondhand criticism usually does not want to be identified as the source of the criticism. While this makes the initiator of the criticism more comfortable, it creates havoc for you, the recipient.

By not taking responsibility for the criticism, the giver has changed the nature of criticism process. It is no longer a direct interaction; instead, you are dealing with a surrogate who cannot clarify your questions and may or may not be giving the criticism accurately, thus making the information passed on to you suspect. For these reasons, the common response to secondhand criticism is anger and a feeling of helplessness, which typically cause the recipient to assume a defensive posture. (Criticism through e-mail or letter is different in that you eventually have the opportunity to respond directly to the original source of the criticism.)

Nevertheless, if you are the recipient of secondhand criticism, you can still benefit. Here are four ways:

1. Assume an investigative stance rather than a defensive one. Assess the validity of the second party. Is he really reliable? Can you trust him? Do you have reason to doubt what he is saying? Thank him for the information, and express appreciation for his not sharing it with others. (You have no control over whether he actually does share it, so your best strategy is to communicate your expectation that he will keep it between the two of you.)
2. If the second party will not identify the source of the criticism, encourage him to ask his source to speak to you directly.
3. Go to your supervisor and explain that you have heard criticism about yourself. Ask her for her advice about how you can find the source of the criticism. This step is a bit tricky because you would not want to incriminate yourself with your boss by letting her know you may be doing something that others think is negative. Therefore, you need to consider this step

in the context of the relationship you have with your boss. If you know she will support you, take it. If not, be careful.
4. Most important, appraise the validity of the criticism. If it's valid, forget about the source and take the necessary productive actions. If you do, you get the power of positive criticism.

What about using secondhand criticism to your advantage? Sometimes, criticizing a person can be a healthy way to go about business. If, for example, you believe your criticism will not be taken well by your recipient, or that it will take on more power by having it delivered by a different source, then you might be wise to criticize your recipient to an individual who you believe can carry on the task for you. It might also be that you have little access to your recipient so you need someone to pass on the information. Whatever the situation, to use secondhand criticism productively, you must let your surrogate know that if the recipient asks, you take full responsibility for the criticism and will be happy to directly discuss the matter.

Unfortunately, this advice taking of responsibility for the criticism is not practiced widely by organizations. Case in point is the ever-growing popular 360 degree assessment in which information about an individual is gathered from a variety of people—subordinates, coworkers, boss, clients— and then funneled back to the individual through a facilitator.

While it is always a smart practice to get multiple sources of information for any evaluation (it increases the reliability of the judgment), the problem in the process of most 360s is that it encourages irresponsible communication by not having every person take responsibility for the criticisms they are giving; their identity is kept anonymous, thus allowing them to say whatever they please because they have the cloak of anonymity to shield them and their criticism. In effect, irresponsible communication is promoted. This is a problem because crucial to productive communication in a relationship or organization is that people take responsibility for their thoughts and feelings.

A psychology graduate department handled the 360 differently. In their case, students have to pass comprehensive exams for their Ph.D. preparation. Every teacher reads the exams and passes their evaluation to the student's adviser, who is responsible for passing it on to the student. During the evaluation, the student is told who said what and is mandated to speak to each teacher directly. In essence, this process promotes responsible communication because it requires that every evaluator take responsibility for their criticisms and, by doing so, encourages that criticism be given directly and openly. The school reports that it is a very growth-oriented process, whereas most folks say 360s aren't.

In the end, your goal for dealing with secondhand criticism is to diminish it so that criticism can be an open, productive, and direct process. Taking responsibility for what you say and encouraging those you work with to criticize you directly will help you achieve this goal and, in the process, get more positive power from criticism.

I Knew Him When . . .

It is almost inevitable. You (or someone you have worked with for quite a while) will be promoted and, as a result, will be a boss (or a subordinate). People find this to be a difficult situation because the change in work status changes the relationship they have with their coworker. If they are the newly appointed boss, they have greater responsibility and authority; with those two job attributes, they are also expected to criticize (evaluate) their subordinate. The problem is, the subordinate used to be their former coworker; in that relationship, they may have given very little or very subtle criticism to the individual. Now, they can be more frequent and direct. This is a big change, one that the former coworker usually does not appreciate.

Similarly, if your former coworker is now your boss, you will be getting more criticism from someone who perhaps rarely disclosed his perceptions as to how you were doing. You will probably be surprised and taken aback as you now find out how he really evaluates you. On the flip side, perhaps you and your coworker criticized each other productively. Now that he is your boss, he may not be as open to your criticism as you had thought.

There are other possibilities too, but the point to recognize is that it is these changing relationship issues that make this situation troublesome for so many people. The strategy you select will obviously depend on whether the change in the relationship makes you the subordinate or the boss.

If you have become the subordinate, you should do nothing differently. You have already developed a style of relating to your former coworker, and there is no reason to change it just because she is now your boss. If you perceive that her style of relating to you has changed, that she has become more power-oriented, then you should develop your skill in criticizing upward. Do not confront your new boss and tell her how she has changed because she is sure to attribute your comments, even if accurate, to envy.

The same basic strategy holds true if you become the boss. If your style of criticizing your coworker has been effective, continue doing what works. However, if there has been conflict or disagreement, instead of having to settle for the standstill that is frequently the result of peer criticism, you now have the work power to ensure the results you want. The mistake that most newly appointed bosses make is to force their subordinates to change simply because they are now the boss. In other words, they abuse their power.

A more effective means of handling disagreements is to explain to your former coworker that you certainly respect his views but that you are now accountable for the results. Therefore, it is your responsibility to make the decision you think is best. In effect, what you have done is shift the emphasis from having power to taking responsibility.

A superb execution of this strategy was used by a staff writer for a network television series. After working as a staff writer for two and a half years, he was promoted to producer, which granted him more authority, including the first level of script approval. When one of his former coworkers finished a rough draft of the following week's script, the new producer made significant changes, which upset the staff writer. They had joined the show together, and the criticized writer was probably envious and angry that he hadn't received the promotion. The producer recounts the conversation that followed:

Staff Writer: Hey, I looked at the changes you made. I don't understand. What is it? You're

Producer: the hotshot producer now and want to take control?

Producer: Are you saying you didn't like the changes? And by the way, you will notice that I didn't say these were final changes. I said for you to think about them and see what you can do with them. Our goal is to get the best script.

Staff Writer: Yea, I know. But still, what is it going to be? Now that you're the producer, I have to run everything by you? First of all, there are a lot of lines that you put in that I think stink, to tell you the truth.

Producer: Good! Make sure you underline them so I can do something about them. You know, you have to realize some things. First, just because I got a promotion doesn't mean I am going to tell you what to do. I have always given you criticism about your work, and you have always criticized my ideas, too. So that's not going to change. What will change is that because I have some authority, I can be more influential with the big boys. Maybe the quality of the show can be elevated to something that will really make a mark on the public. Also, I have worked with you for two and a half years. And I know that you are one of the best in the business. If I have to use my power, if it has to come to that, to make you write your best scripts so that you can get the recognition and bucks that you deserve, then, dammit, I will. And if you want to be

| | upset about that, then fine. My job is to be responsible for the quality of the scripts. And I expect you to be, as you have been in the past, open to my criticisms, and I expect you to continue to criticize my work, whether it's my script work or how I carry out my responsibilities as producer. |
| **Staff Writer:** | All right, all right. If you think I'm so good, maybe you can help me get a promotion too. Now, can we go over the script? |

What made this encounter positive was that the producer did four things. First, he clarified for the recipient his intent of the criticism: to get the best script. Doing this kept the criticism process on track because it put the emphasis on the script rather than on the issue of giving criticism because roles had changed.

Second, when the staff writer began to escalate the encounter into an argument ("There are a lot of lines that you put in that I think stink"), the producer stayed calm. Being of good mind, he then turned the rebuttal criticism into a positive opportunity by encouraging his staff writer to make detailed notes about the lines he questioned so they could be looked at. This type of response kept the situation from escalating into a destructive interaction in which nobody would win.

Third, he artfully made another point by referring to some of the qualities that had made their relationship successful in the past—specifically, their productively criticizing each other—and noting that he expected that this would continue. Thus, he let the staff writer know that he would criticize all of his scripts and, at the same time, pointed out that he had been doing this for two and a half years anyway; it had nothing to do with being a new producer.

Finally, the producer defined his job responsibility and strategically put it into the context of how it could benefit the staff writer by securing more money and more recognition for him.

While this particular encounter probably did not wash away the staff writer's deeper feelings of resentment and envy, it did clear the air and set the stage for a productive working relationship. In fact, several months later, the new producer noted that the creative juices of the show were flowing better than ever and that the staff writer was doing his best work ever. Another month passed, and the staff writer had his contract renewed—ironically, for more money and a new title: coproducer of the show!

It is also interesting to note that some people actually do give more criticism once they are promoted. As a coworker, their criticisms were sparse; now they are abundant. More often than not, I find what explains this increased frequency of criticism is that the promoted individual now feels she has the *right* to criticize; in other words, she sees her promotion as empowering her to criticize. Certainly, this is a positive effect of the promotion because the individual now feels more comfortable in disclosing her thoughts and ideas. If you are the recipient, listen to these thoughts and ideas rather than simply attributing them to her new powerful position. You might get the power of positive criticism.

A Positive Critic

A positive critic, whether giver or taker, is one who can continually get the positive power of criticism. What is special about these people? What are their common denominators? Through years of research, clinical experiences, and training or consulting activities, I have observed five characteristics they share in common.

First is *awareness*—of themselves, of others, and of the importance of criticism. Positive critics are tenaciously looking to increase their awareness of themselves and others. They want information about themselves because they know it will help them navigate through life more effectively. Because they value awareness about themselves, it is natural for them to be receptive to criticism (one of criticism's chief functions is to help you learn about yourself).

Positive critics are also aware of others—their feelings, their emotions, their actions. Their awareness of others gives them valuable information that helps them mold their thoughts into an effective criticism delivery, often on the spur of the moment.

Positive critics also recognize the importance of criticism. They know its role in achieving individual and organizational success. (Note that for positive critics, criticism is their chief tool for increasing self-awareness and their awareness of others. The positive results they attain serve to strengthen their desire for both awareness and criticism.)

Second, positive critics hold a philosophy that advocates that *people are in the process of becoming their best*. This implies that people not only can change but also want to do their best. Out of this philosophy comes the view that criticism is a tool to help people do their best.

Third, the positive critic is *self-responsible.* He acknowledges and acts on the principle that individuals are responsible for their actions. In the case of criticism, he is aware that it is his choice as to how he responds to the criticisms he receives, and his choice as to how he delivers criticism to others. He recognizes that nobody makes him defensive, and nobody forces him to put down others. Because he takes responsibility for how he manages criticism, he is able to consciously choose the most effective ways for dealing with criticisms, both given and received.

Fourth, the positive critic is *active.* Accepting responsibility for her actions catalyzes the positive critic to go looking for ways to make things better. For herself, she actively seeks criticism from others, knowing that this input will increase her awareness and thus help her become more effective. Her behavior matches the attitude of "Please tell me how I can do better. I want to know what you think."

She is also active in searching for ways to help others be their best. She offers criticism to others. Because she values criticism, believes people want to do their best, and sees criticism as a tool to achieve that task, she and her criticisms are perceived by recipients as having positive intent.

Fifth, the positive critic practices positive criticism. He practices what he preaches, and he does this as a culmination of the other characteristics. Through his practicing, he becomes a role model for others around him. He shows how to give and take criticism. Through his practicing of positive criticism, he further increases his awareness of which of his criticism skills can be more finely tuned for greater effectiveness. But most of all, he has learned that it feels good to give and receive the power of positive criticism!

Appendix

The Criticism Inventory (TCI)

The Criticism Inventory has been in existence for over twenty years and is designed to help you clarify your thoughts, feelings, and actions with respect to criticism on the job. From your responses, you will be able to gather information that will help facilitate your skills in giving and taking criticism.

The instrument has been used effectively in diverse settings to help organizations discover the common issues their employees deal with in handling criticism, as well as the most difficult criticisms in their specific organizational culture. Training departments have used the responses to initiate training and development programs as well as to develop content for training and development courses. Customer service departments have found the instrument to be useful in helping their staff anticipate common customer criticisms; thus, they can be better prepared to handle those criticisms when encountered. Team builders have found the instrument to be effective in facilitating team communication as well as developing team criticism skills.

For more information on modifying The Criticism Inventory to meet your needs, or for information on its application, contact the author.

The Criticism Inventory

Please respond to the following questions in as much detail as possible. Studying your responses will provide you with valuable information in helping you develop your skills for giving and taking criticism.

1. Write your definition of "criticism":

_____

_____

_____

2. Rate your comfort/discomfort level in *giving* criticism:

1	2	3	4	5	6	7	8	9

very comfortable   very uncomfortable

3. Rate your comfort/discomfort level in *taking* criticism:

1	2	3	4	5	6	7	8	9

very comfortable   very uncomfortable

4. What makes it difficult for you to *give* criticism at work:

_____

_____

5. What makes it difficult for you to *take* criticism at work:

_____

_____

6. The most difficult criticism for me to *give* is:

_____

_____

Reason: _____

_____

7. The most difficult criticism for me to *receive* is:

_____

_____

Reason: _____

_____

8. The person whom it is most difficult for me to criticize is:

_____

Reason: _____

_____

9. The person whom it is most difficult for me to receive criticism from is:

_____

Reason: _____

_____

10. I find it hardest to criticize my (subordinate/peer/supervisor).
I find it easiest to criticize my (subordinate/peer/superior).

Reason: _____

_____

11. I find it hardest to receive criticism from my (subordinate/peer/superior). I find it easiest to receive criticism from my (subordinate/peer/superior).

Reason: _____

_____

_____

12. Who is most and least responsive to my work criticism:

_____

Reason: _____

_____

_____

13. Any other thoughts you would like to share about criticism:

_____

_____

_____

Index

About the Author

Hendrie Weisinger, Ph.D., is a licensed psychologist with extensive experience in clinical, counseling, and organizational psychology. He is a leading authority in the application of Emotional Intelligence, an expert in Anger Management, and the originator of the highly regarded techniques of Criticism Training.

Dr. Weisinger is the author of several successful books, including *Emotional Intelligence at Work, Dr. Weisinger's Anger Workout Book, Anger at Work,* and the *New York Times* bestseller, *Nobody's Perfect.* He has made more than 500 appearances on major television news and information programs including *Oprah, Good Morning America,* and *The Today Show.* His work has been featured in numerous newspapers and national magazines, including *The New York Times* Sunday Business section, *USA Today,* and *Business Week.* His article for *The Wall Street Journal,* "So You're Afraid to Criticize Your Boss," was selected as one of the sixty best articles to appear in the "Manager's Column," and is reprinted in *The Wall Street Journal on Management,* published by Dow Jones. His article for *TV Guide,* "Tutored by Television," is being read into *The Congressional Record.*

Dr. Weisinger's expertise has been sought by dozens of Fortune 500 companies, government agencies, school systems, hospitals and mental health agencies, educational associations, and The Young Presidents Organization.

Dr. Weisinger currently teaches in a number of executive education and MBA programs, including Wharton, Cornell, MIT, NYU, Rensselaer Polytechnic Institute, Wake Forest, and Penn State.

Contact Information

If you are interested in having Dr. Weisinger speak or consult to your organization, you may contact him at:

The Learning Circle
978-461-9929